GLORIOUS HOPE

GLORIOUS HOPE

Stories of Life, Faith, and Finishing Well

Editors of Guideposts

Guideposts
New York

Acknowledgments

Every attempt has been made to credit the sources of copyrighted material used in this book. If any such acknowledgment has been inadvertently omitted or miscredited, receipt of such information would be appreciated.

All Scripture quotations unless otherwise indicated are taken from the Holy Bible, New International Version®, NIV® Copyright © 1973, 1978, 1984, 2011 by Biblica, Inc.™ Used by permission. All rights reserved worldwide.

Scripture quotations marked (ESV) are taken from the *Holy Bible, English Standard Version*, copyright © 2001 by Crossway Bibles, a division of Good News Publishers. Used by permission. All rights reserved.

Scripture quotations marked (KJV) are taken from *The King James Version of the Bible*.

Scripture quotations marked (RSV) are taken from the *Revised Standard Version of the Bible*. Copyright © 1946, 1952, 1971 by Division of Christian Education of the National Council of Churches of Christ in the U.S.A. Used by permission.

Cover and interior design by Müllerhaus
Cover image provided by Shutterstock
Typesetting by Aptara, Inc.

Printed and bound in the United States of America
10 9 8 7 6 5 4 3

CONTENTS

CHAPTER 6: SERVE . . . and Tap In to God's Strength

Afterword

INTRODUCTION

Hope—glorious hope! It's what keeps us going when a situation is not easy; it's what we cling to when circumstances are not certain.

Dr. Norman Vincent Peale, pastor and founder of Guideposts, says, "Hope is more than just a word; it's a dynamic force, a concept full of power. It can bring the weak back to strength. It can bring the sick back to health. It can turn failure into success. No wonder St. Paul placed it with the three great principles of Christianity: faith, hope, and love."

The Bible tells us that God has a vision for each of us, plans for "a future and a hope." That sounds on target for someone in their twenties and thirties...but how about those of us in our sixties, seventies, eighties, and nineties? Does God still have a plan for us in our later years?

This is the question we explored for this book. What we found surprised us. It was that the very act of hoping—of having faith that God has a purpose for our later years—produces a kind of transforming strength of its own.

Glorious Hope reveals the surprising spiritual strength that builds when we face the challenges of aging with God's hope in our hearts. You will see yourself—and find positive new perspective on your situation—in over three-dozen stories from people in their later years.

John Sherrill realizes God has a continuing purpose for him as he watches an old candle and a new one burn side by side—and notes that both give out the same amount of light. Marjorie Holmes takes you through the surprising circumstances that led to her later-in-life second marriage, and her discovery that our ability to love—and be loved—remains unchanged. Mary Ann O'Roark reveals how the realities of aging made her feel alone and unsure...until a chance meeting with a movie star she admired showed her that true beauty comes from a wellspring of inner grace.

Many other contributors acknowledge the surprising kindling of spiritual strength that happens amid fading physical strength. Their gracious, thoughtful insights remind us that although our physical bodies creak and sag, our spirits remain alert, active, and intact, and that God has a plan that goes beyond our physical existence.

May the God of hope fill you with all joy and peace as you trust in Him.

—Editors of Guideposts

1 HOPE . . . BELIEVE GOD HAS A PURPOSE FOR YOU

For I know the plans I have for you, declares the Lord,
plans for welfare and not for evil,
to give you a future and a hope.

—JEREMIAH 29:11 (ESV)

IN THE FULLNESS OF TIME by Dora Flack

My husband and I planted that tree thirty years ago when we first moved into our new home. It was a young shoot of a peach tree, just beginning. Kind of like us.

I watched it from the kitchen window of our brick rambler. I watched it filling out and growing strong as I baked bread and prepared breakfasts and suppers for my husband, LeGrand, and our little ones. They came like the peaches on that tree—one, two, three sons; then one, two, three daughters. Babies, tender and pink, with peach fuzz on their heads. And I watched them filling out and growing strong.

Each year we gave our tree a good measure of tender loving care; each year it gave back to us.

"Just look, Dora." My husband pointed to its branches. "It's already bearing peaches. And here, it's only the second year."

"Yes!" I counted excitedly, "One, two, three, four, five, six" small green balls that reddened and ripened by late summer. Just enough for our cereal topping.

3

Each year LeGrand trimmed and fed and pruned our tree. By its fourth year it was giving so much fruit that we feared its young branches would snap from the weight. From that time, each June I thinned the hard, green, developing peaches while LeGrand worried: "Dora, you're going to ruin that tree with your merciless thinning!"

But each harvest seemed more bountiful. So bountiful that after several weeks of peaches and cream, peach pies and peach ice cream, there were plenty to can for the winter months. Still there were bushels more, too many for even our large family. Those bushels we gave away.

"Another record harvest!" LeGrand would say. "Ten bushels again."

"How can it keep on giving so much?" I wondered out loud.

"Well, we take good care of it," LeGrand reminded me. "And maybe it has something to do with our giving those peaches away."

Just like the Giving Tree, I thought, noting that sometimes one or two of my fresh loaves of bread seemed more than we needed. I'd look out at the Giving Tree and send one of the children to deliver the loaves to neighbors.

Our children grew strong and healthy, but just like our tree, they had to fight off the inevitable diseases—measles, chicken pox, flu. Sometimes I'd be up in the middle of the night with a feverish child.

Then it came my time. I had a long spell with a bad back and had to be doctored and nurtured back to health.

And then our tree. Borers worked their way into its bark at the base. LeGrand carefully dug out the larvae and treated the damaged area with a solution from the nursery. "It'll soon be healthy again," he promised. And it was. Just as we all had recovered and gone about our tasks again. The Giving Tree continued giving peaches.

Then one winter morning following a heavy snowstorm, I heard a strange groan, almost human. Looking up from my dishwashing, I glanced out the window to see a big bare branch of our Giving Tree slowly bending and then sinking to the ground, leaving a jagged opening in the trunk. I could almost feel the cold hit the inner heart of the tree.

"Oh dear." I sighed. "Our lovely old tree is beginning to give in to age and the elements. It's downhill from here, I guess."

I complained through the next two years when other branches broke off, just as I did when I observed age catching up with LeGrand and me—dimming eyesight, weakening and sagging here and there.

"Dora," LeGrand would tell me, "no tree lasts indefinitely. Just like us."

But each summer it seemed the remaining branches continued to bear fruit with greater determination. And we continued to share its peaches and the pies and jars of jam that we made.

Then late one summer I called to LeGrand, "The tree's leaning precariously. We'd better give it some supports."

LeGrand propped the heavily laden branches of the Giving Tree. Its peaches were turning gold and red but were not yet ripe enough for picking.

"I hope that'll support the poor old tree for just one more harvest," he said.

The following evening the tree's limbs swayed and shuddered with an early fall wind. Lightning streaked through ominous clouds. Dismayed, I watched leaves and twigs driven through the air.

"This will surely drive the tree down," I worried out loud. "If we could just get this crop," I said wistfully.

"How much can you expect of that poor old tree?" my husband replied. "I wish I could get you as interested in the rest of the garden."

But the limbs, bowed with ripening fruit, swayed with the props and remained upright.

By this time, our children had left home. They were settling into their own homes, starting families, taking root nearby. LeGrand and I were grandparents and proud of the little "shoots" sprouting in our own family.

Finally, in its twenty-sixth year, the Giving Tree had lost all of its branches. Only a bare three-foot-high stump remained.

"I'd better get that ugly old stump out this fall so we can plant a new peach tree next spring," my husband said.

"I hate to see it go," I replied. "It's given so much."

Early winter storms prevented LeGrand's digging out the stump.

The next spring, a small shoot emerged from the dark, scarred bark just a few inches from where the last branch had dropped off.

"LeGrand, that tree's determined to keep giving!" I exclaimed happily.

"Would you look at that," he said with a whistle.

Our kids and grandchildren watched eagerly as the shoot grew into a healthy branch. "Do you think there will be peaches, Grandma?" they wanted to know.

None came that year. But they came the next when the new shoot grew into a new tree. It emerged from the old stump even though the bark was breaking away and the wood inside was rotting.

"The trunk will never last this season," LeGrand declared.

But it did. "Amazing!" we agreed.

That old peach tree became my symbol of productive longevity. It could still give a heavy harvest even though its feet were crumbling—just as mine and LeGrand's were beginning to hurt.

The following spring, the stump sounded hollow to the tap. At the ground line it seemed ready to topple at the slightest push. But the new limbs were covered with delicate pink blossoms.

"Anything trying so hard to live should live," LeGrand and I decided.

This was a difficult year. LeGrand had a heart attack; I was struggling with a serious eye problem. But as I thinned back the green peaches that summer and watched the velvet, juicy fruit developing, enough for LeGrand and me, enough for our children and their children, I thought of those words in the Bible that tell us "Every good tree bringeth forth good fruit. . . . Wherefore by their fruits ye shall know them" (Matthew 7:17, 20, KJV).

The same was true of LeGrand and me. We still had nourishing things to give, despite our age, despite our lessening strength.

LeGrand could still give from his garden—to friends, to the sick, to those in need. I could do the same with my baked goods.

LeGrand, just retired from his accounting work, finds time for volunteer computer work at church and for other service. He loves studying hard to teach the adult class in Sunday school each week. I still lecture widely to state and local groups. I still sing and give book reviews and write and teach at church. There is no end to one-on-one assistance for friends and neighbors.

And there are our children and our twenty-one "shoots"—all in need of a little nurturing now and then. We love it because, like the tree, giving has become our life. Like the tree, we can find new life in our aging bodies, and in doing so, we can continue to give—even in the coming years when LeGrand and I, too, may have to be supported by props.

A CIRCLE OF LIGHT by John Sherrill

I followed the choir out of the stalls singing "Joy to the World." We filed out of the church, decorated for Christmas Eve with candles, flowers, and evergreen branches. In the changing room, I swapped season's greetings with friends.

My cheerfulness, however, was a bit forced. I'd sung in this choir for forty-five years, and tonight my age had begun to show, my voice breaking like a teenager's. *I should step aside,* I thought. *Older people are furloughed elsewhere. Why should church be different?*

I joined my wife, Tib, and we drove home, to our living room where grandchildren's stockings lay on the sofa, and boxes tumbled out from under the tree. On the coffee table was my wreath, which I'd forgotten to put away now that Advent was over. I looked at the four small candles, lighted one by one on Sunday mornings over the past weeks. They made a staircase now, from oldest to youngest, the first candle little more than a mound of wax lumped around a blackened wick.

I was about to pull the candles out of the wreath when, on impulse, I found a match and lit the oldest. The ravaged candle began to give its light. I stopped, transfixed, struck another match and lit the second candle. Then I lit the third and fourth. Each candle, young or old, gave the same amount of light.

A physical light, of course, but more. The candles also brought radiance from beyond, speaking as they did of attributes of the Christmas mystery: hope and love, joy and peace. That's what the choir—indeed, any outreach of the church—should be doing: showcasing each believer's unique light, a light that had little to do with age or talent. In that moment I knew that I would continue to sing. Quietly perhaps, but as long as I could, I would definitely continue to sing.

OUR WRITERS' GROUP by Gina Bridgeman

For several years, I've participated in a writers' group once a month. I critique their work, answer questions, and offer advice on getting published. I try to encourage the members as much as

I can. They're quite prolific; they often send their work to magazine and book editors, and enter contests. Some have seen their prose in print, and others have finished ambitious memoirs they're trying to get published.

Why is this group so special? Every member is over the age of eighty. Their founder is still writing poetry at ninety-five. They inspire me because they all have dreams—of writing a good story, seeing it published, and sharing it with others. And aside from the occasional jokes about fading memory and bifocals, they don't see their age as an obstacle to achieving their dreams. In fact, as each day passes, they continue to use the gifts God has given them. Age is never an issue.

Thanks to these friends, I'm filled with hope when I try to picture myself twice the age I am now. I don't fear growing older because I've seen that enthusiasm and good humor can help keep my spirit young. Also, I know that God will still have work for me. I think of others whom God put to work in their later years: biblical heroes like Noah and Moses, and more recent heroes like Mother Teresa and the Reverend Billy Graham. As my own parents continue to work and volunteer, I see firsthand that God will have plenty for me to do as long as I'm healthy and my spirit is willing to follow where He leads me.

HAPPY 100TH by Willard Scott

One hundred. Who lives to be one hundred? Lots of people, in fact. In the years I've been celebrating centenarians on the *Today* show, thousands of them have sent me letters. They write to me about their lives, loves, passions, dreams. Initially, I had thought of them as curiosities, as unusual as a man seven feet tall. Not anymore. Along the way, I noticed commonalities about these remarkable folks. I began to change my own habits to conform to theirs. I lost weight. I began exercising. I treated each day as a gift. I wanted what they had.

The hundred-year-olds I talk to don't claim some secret formula. Most will say they eat right, stay fit, practice moderation. Some say they have good genes. Most say faith in God plays a big part. But what strikes me is this: By and large, they are the most positive people I have ever known. Age and infirmity haven't dampened their zest for living. There's the 101-year-old man who walks a half mile each day. The 107-year-old woman who never misses a Red Sox game. The former Ziegfeld Follies star who still dances. These folks also exercise their minds. They play pinochle and Scrabble. They complete the newspaper crossword puzzles. They never fail to marvel at how the world has changed. And they'd love to tell you about it.

If you know one of these people, seek her out. Let her talk. You'll hear more than mere history. You'll be handed a roadmap to a life well lived.

A NOVEL TURN by Effie Leland Wilder

I've been at the Presbyterian Home of South Carolina in Summerville for eleven years now. They've been good years, for the most part. I'll be honest, though—life in a retirement home took some getting used to. And it took even longer for me to appreciate it. I had expected all that, but I had never dreamed living here would be the start of a literary career.

When I came, I had been on my own for eight years, ever since my husband, Frank, died. I did all right at first—even took a liking to my independence. As I got on in years, however, the big old house became too much for me to manage all alone. I didn't want to burden my children with making room for me, so I decided to move into a retirement home.

Closing up the house where I had spent more than half my life was the worst trauma I have ever experienced. Memories hit me with every drawer and closet I cleaned out; it seemed as if I were throwing away my life and my family's lives.

As I emptied the shelves in the den, I pictured Frank there with our daughter, Frances, on her birthday, putting a ruler on her head and carefully marking her height on the back of the door. She and our three boys always got a kick out of seeing how much they had grown since the year before. It nearly did me in to shut that door for the last time.

I got through pitching and packing, finally, and moved my things into the Presbyterian Home. I have my own cottage here, and my children made it snug and cozy, decorating the rooms, planting azaleas to brighten up the tiny lawn. They even managed to squeeze my baby grand piano into the living room.

I'm grateful I had my music those first months. I needed something familiar. There was so much to adjust to. For instance, when living alone, I had eaten when the mood struck me, but here, meals are on a regular schedule. After missing breakfast twice in three days, I wondered, *Am I ever going to get used to this place?* Feeling out of sorts, I sat down at my piano with my Chopin nocturnes. The keys were cool beneath my fingertips, and as I played those lilting melodies, I felt a little like I was at home again.

Gradually, I settled into the routine and got to know the other folks. Some things about this place are even better than being at my own house. There's always someone around to laugh or commiserate with, to play cards or watch old movies with. The best part is, when people talk about Ronald Colman or Lum 'n' Abner or Lydia Pinkham or Studebakers, they don't have to pause and explain.

The understanding doesn't stop there. One day I got to missing my Frank, and it must have showed, because at lunch my friends asked me why I was being so quiet. "It's silly," I told them. "You'll laugh at me."

"Try us."

"All right," I said. "I was dusting this morning when the cloth just came apart in my hands." I felt tears pricking at my eyelids. "You see, it was Frank's old undershirt—the last one I have. He always told me not to throw them out. Said they'd make great dusters. And now he's gone . . . and they're gone . . . and I'm crying over an old dust rag." I couldn't go on.

No one laughed. One of the ladies gently laid her hand on my arm, and the others chatted, letting me have a minute to compose myself.

When I got back to my cottage later, I just couldn't get that bittersweet moment out of my mind. So I put my thoughts down on paper, in the notepad where I had been jotting down some of the funny things I had heard in the dining room. I wasn't quite certain why I had started doing it, except I surely enjoy a good chuckle, and Lord knows, sometimes I needed one.

Well, I enjoy writing, I thought as I flipped through the notebook. *Maybe I need to keep doing it.* I hadn't had much opportunity since my days in the literary society at Converse College. Now, of course, I had plenty.

I found myself filling notebook after notebook with the goings-on around this place. Most of my jottings were of the amusing sort. Life in an old folks' home—and I venture to say, life in general—would be pretty miserable without a sense of humor. My friend Mary, in particular, can find a joke in almost any situation. She walks around wearing a sweatshirt with the message, "You know you're getting old when the Happy Hour is a nap!"

Sometimes the experiences I wrote about were poignant. As I was going to visit a friend in the infirmary one afternoon, a woman stopped me in the hallway. "Honey, can you tell me how to get where I'm goin'?" she asked.

"Where are you trying to go?"

"I don't know," she answered cheerfully. "They haven't told me yet."

Then there's the gentleman who, at age ninety, was told he needed a pacemaker. The doctors explained his options: a device that would last ten years or a more-expensive model that might last twenty years. He went for the latter, God bless him.

I would have kept my writing to myself if my daughter, Frances, hadn't happened to pick up one of my notebooks. After reading a few pages, she looked at me eagerly. "Mother, these notes are funny, really funny," she said. "You should put them into a book."

"What kind of a book?" The thought had never crossed my mind.

"How about a novel? You could call it *Life Among the Wheelchairs*."

I took umbrage at that. "Very few of us are in wheelchairs," I retorted. "And even if we were, I'd still have to have some kind of a plot."

That night I went to bed pondering what Frances had said. *Lord, I thought, what's interesting enough for me to build a story around?* Suddenly I thought of Henry, a nice young man who works in our maintenance department. He's sharp, but he has dyslexia and never learned to read well enough to take the written part of the driver's license test. A friend here—a retired schoolteacher—had started tutoring him, and in a few months Henry had his license.

I asked Henry if he would mind my writing a story about him. He graciously gave his permission. I had my starting point, and I was off. I wrote the novel in about five weeks, based on the real-life happenings I had jotted down in my notebooks. Frances loved it and urged me to get it published. I had done a few articles for the *Charleston News and Courier*, and once—a long way back—I had sold a story to *The Saturday Evening Post*, but I didn't know a thing about book publishing.

Still, I sent my manuscript to a publisher in North Carolina. They rejected it politely. I hesitated about sending it anywhere else, but a friend insisted I try Peachtree Publishers in Atlanta. I put it in the mail and said a prayer.

Weeks went by without a word. Then one day I got a letter from their managing editor. They were interested in my book and wanted to know more about me! I phoned the editor and told him a bit about myself. Soon after that, the editor called to tell me they were going to publish my book. My novel, *Out to Pasture (But Not Over the Hill)*, came out in 1995 and was quite a success.

All my friends here at the Presbyterian Home were excited about the book. Just as wonderful, I heard from hundreds of strangers who said they were touched by it. Several people told me I made their decision to go into a retirement home a little easier. I guess it's like the Good Book says in Psalm 92:3–14. Those who are "planted in the house of the Lord, they will flourish.... They will still bear fruit in old age, they will stay fresh and green."

To have something I started for my own enjoyment end up reaching so many folks, well, that is surely a blessing. Or, as I like to think, it's God's icing on the cake of my life.

THE MAN WHO WANTED TO GO HOME
by Jimmy Gupton

Another Christmas coming...toy commercials and holiday specials on television. And here I was, an old man spending another evening in front of the tube.

Why, Lord? I asked for the thousandth time. *Why won't You just go ahead and take me home?*

I had been a Christian all my life and figured the Almighty didn't mind my taking a familiar tone with Him. *Ninety-three years is long enough on this earth. I've lived a full life, and I can't see how I'm much good to You or anyone else anymore.*

When my wife was alive, it was different. But Bess had been gone seven years, and for me, it was getting harder to go through the motions. Christmas, for example. I hadn't even bothered to get the big silver tree out of the box in the attic this year. It was a pretty thing, but attaching 150 branches was a big job. After my eyes went bad I'd had to take an ice pick to feel for the holes. *With only me here, why bother?*

A rock group came on the TV to sing "Jingle Bells." *You see, Lord, I'm not going to be able to take care of this place much longer, and You know I don't want to go somewhere else.* My two sons and their families kept asking me to move in with one of them, but I'm a stubborn kind of fellow. I liked my independence.

This past year, though . . . It was a small house, but it was getting to be too much. The roof was leaking, the wallpaper peeling. *Why can't I just come home, Lord, and not fool with an interim move?*

On the TV screen flashed pictures of the Salvation Army shelter in downtown Charlotte, part of a series on homelessness at Christmas. "There are over two hundred women sleeping here tonight," an announcer said, "out of work and out of hope." I sure felt sorry for those people. But I hardly had enough money to cover my own expenses, much less make a donation. At about ten o'clock I switched off the set, turned off the lights and said my usual prayers before climbing into bed.

Instead of falling asleep, though, I kept seeing those women at the shelter. I had always given to the poor when I was able. Surely it was someone else's turn. But that news report wouldn't let me alone. There were those women needing help. *Just like me,* I thought.

I sat up in bed. *What if two needy folks were to put their needs together? What if one of those women were to move in, take care of the house in exchange for a place to live?*

The next morning I telephoned the shelter. "If you're serious, Mr. Gupton," the manager said, "I'll ask around."

A few days after Christmas, he called back. "Would you consider taking in a married couple?"

"Well, now . . ." I hadn't counted on two people. "It's such a small house," I apologized. "The spare room's barely big enough for one."

"What I was thinking," the man went on, "was that the wife could keep house, and the husband could look after the yard. As for the size of the room, I'm sure anything with a door would look like a palace to them right now." The manager paused a moment to let that sink in. "I think I've got the perfect couple. Tony and Pam Davis." Both had lost their jobs. Unable to meet rent payments, they had been evicted from their home and ended up sleeping at the shelter at night and job hunting during the day. "It's hard to impress an employer when you're wearing wrinkled clothing and have no permanent address."

"Send them over," I said. "We'll give it a try."

It looked as though it was going to work. Pam was a little shy at first, but before the week was out we were chatting like old friends. She told me she had been a waitress and Tony had worked as a carpet installer, until both places of employment went out of business the same month. With downcast eyes, she described what it had been like to be in a Salvation Army shelter at Christmastime.

It was nice to have someone keeping house, cooking meals, taking care of the yard again. Wonderful to have them care enough to escort me to the senior citizens' center, to drive me to church.

About three months after they had come, though, Pam said she needed to talk to me. The two of us had just finished lunch. Tony had found a job with another carpet-installation company and was gone during the day.

"I don't know how to say this, Mr. Gupton," she began.

Oh no! I thought. *She's going to tell me they're moving out now that Tony's working.*

Pam got up and started piling dishes in the sink. "I know I should have told you in the beginning," she said, "but I was afraid you wouldn't let us stay—and you might want us to leave after you hear this. But I can't put off telling you any longer...."

She twisted the dishrag in her hands. "You see, I...I'm"— she lifted her dark eyes to stare into mine—"I'm going to have a baby."

So that was it! "Well, you're right about one thing," I said. "I hadn't counted on three of you, that's for sure." She turned away, looking down at the sink. "But I certainly can't let you go back on the streets," I assured her. "Not with a baby coming." I tried to keep my voice calm, but my mind was shouting, *A baby! Where will we put a baby?*

"I know there's not much room here," Pam said, as if reading my thoughts. "But if we move the dresser out of our room, I'm sure we could squeeze a small crib in, and I'll try to keep the baby quiet so it won't disturb you."

I nodded. "I'm sure we'll manage," I said. "Don't you worry."

The months flew by. Pam shifted the tiny room around and sandwiched a crib between the bed and the wall, bought diapers and bottles, and began a whirlwind of painting and wallpapering all over the house.

And before I knew it, a redheaded baby girl named Sabrina arrived. Pam tried to keep her quiet and out of my way. Soon she was three months old, then five months old, and then it was the middle of December—almost Christmas again.

I was sitting in the living room one evening, reading the second chapter of Luke, as I always did at this time of year. "And she brought forth her firstborn son," I read, "and laid him in a manger; because there was no room for them in the inn" (Luke 2:7, KJV).

That must have saddened God, I thought, feeling pretty good that I had found room for the Davis family, though in some ways it had been an inconvenience. Even as I thought about the crowded inn, though, I knew that wasn't the point of the story. What God had wanted, far more than a room at the inn, was for people to open their hearts and make room for His Son.

Perhaps that's what He had been trying to get me to do. Sure, I had made room for the Davises in my house, but maybe God had been trying to get me to make room in my heart.

The winter wind was beating at the windows, seeping around the newspapers Pam had stuffed into the cracks. I got up and stoked the fire in the woodstove; had to keep the place warm for the baby. *You know,* I told myself, *if we slid the couch back against the wall, I believe there'd be room for a playpen in here. Can't keep a growing child cooped up in a bedroom.*

I walked over to the stairs. "Tony! Pam!" I called.

"What is it, Mr. Gupton?" Tony asked, hurrying down.

"Is something wrong?" asked Pam, following behind him, alarm in her eyes.

"You bet something's wrong," I said. "Here it is almost Christmas, and we don't have a tree up!"

"We thought about that," Tony admitted. "But trees are so expensive."

"That's so," I agreed. "But I happen to know where there's a beautiful tree just waiting to be put up. It's in a box in the attic now, but when it's standing tall and grand with the colored lights beaming from its silver branches, why, you never saw anything so pretty in all your life. With a child in the house, we've got to have a Christmas tree!"

Tony and Pam raced up the rickety stairs to the attic and dragged down the bulky box. Pam unpacked the branches; I fluffed the needles and passed them to Tony to insert in the holes. It was fun doing it together. I coached Tony as he set the tree in the revolving stand I had made out of an old TV antenna many years before. Then I switched on the multicolored floodlight and sat back to enjoy their *oohs* and *aahs* as the tree started to turn like a silver ballerina.

About that time, we heard a hungry wail from upstairs. Pam ran up and brought Sabrina down. Pam looked surprised but pleased when I motioned for her to hand the baby to me while she went off to the kitchen to heat a bottle. We sat there eyeing each other silently. I felt kind of awkward.

Sabrina studied my face intently, and for a moment I thought she was going to cry. But instead she broke into a laugh and reached a chubby little hand toward my cheek. I laughed too when I realized she was trying to catch the fleeting reflections from the tree. The touch of her hand made me think of another Child, born on Christmas so many years ago.

I looked at Tony arranging candles in the window, listened to Pam humming a carol in the kitchen. And I whispered a prayer to the One Who has our times in His keeping, "Thank You, Lord, for letting me see another Christmas...for leaving me here though I fussed and fretted. Sometimes it takes a baby to remind an old man what Your world is all about."

ON THE WAY TO CODY by Don Bell

Lately I've had trouble with my eyes. I've lost all sight in my right eye, and now the left one is clouding up. The doctor says there's not much can be done. Some days I feel pretty hopeless because of this. I sit outside or by the window and wonder how much longer I'll see the land. I'm an old guy, seventy-four, and it's often hard for me to believe there's cause for hope waiting down my road. But I ought to remember the mysterious music that came drifting across a bleak plain during another bleak period in my life.

It was a time when winter was just coming on, and I was in a little Montana town called Belfry. The cattle had been brought down to winter pasture. As a cowhand, I had only one big task remaining, and that was to drive the saddle horses home to a winter range near Cody, Wyoming, forty miles to the south.

The year was 1953, when the high plains along the Montana–Wyoming border were still pretty wild. My trip home wasn't that long in miles, but it would take me down a wilderness road. No lodgings. No homesteads.

You always worry when you go down a deserted road. When the weather turns terrible, you really begin to doubt. That morning in Belfry, the wind came howling from the north, driving the winter's first snow before it. But I had to start home, or my string would be stuck in Montana until spring.

I dressed in all the clothes a human could possibly wear and still ride a horse. I bought a sack lunch at the Belfry Café, stashed it in my slicker, and then tied the whole bundle behind my saddle's cantle. Good-bye, Montana.

My thirty horses had already started home for Wyoming. They knew the way, drawn homeward the way rivers are drawn to the sea. I followed all day, buttons fastened and collars turned up, glad to have the snow at my back.

Toward dusk, I caught up with my string. They looked at first like horses in a dream, barely visible, cloaked in driving snow. No sound except the wind. My own saddle horse called to those ahead. A few turned. We all kept moving.

The going had been slower than I'd expected. I'd saved my lunch because I didn't want to eat too early in the trip, but now I was fiercely hungry. Time for lunch and supper. I reached back. That's funny. I patted around. The bundle was gone. It had probably snagged in a willow branch . . . way too many miles ago.

Nothing to eat and still a long way to travel, thirty miles I figured. All along I'd known I might have to ride much of the night, but hadn't banked on doing it with an empty stomach.

I rode all humped up to hold on to my warmth. Nobody lived along this road. No shelters either. I had to keep riding. I had no choice. I beat my cold hands against my stiffened chaps. Every few miles, I dismounted and jumped around, trying to stir my blood.

The night seemed endless. At last I sent a prayer through the snow. "Oh, Lord, I need shelter...need it real quick." I made this prayer with all my might, but feared it was pointless. I already knew there wasn't even a convenient cave between here and Cody. I rode on. How much farther? No idea anymore—the lay of the dark land lost to me. I just followed my string. My senses were starting to fail. My eyes would close and I'd begin to drift, I'd dream that daytime—and warmth—had come, and suddenly my saddle would shift and I'd awaken to the same cold night.

And then it happened that I awoke to something strange. Music! I began hearing snatches of songful sound. They came and went with the wind. So it seemed. But how could there be music way out here on the Cody road on so terrible a night? "Must just be the wind," I said to myself. *Or maybe you're really losing your mind.* I kept on. The music, though, kept coming and going. Was there a voice in it?

At last it grew constant, and just then the sound led my eyes to a light. To a bright hole filled with swirling snow. I drew nearer and finally saw that this was lantern-glow from a shepherd's wagon.

I let out a joyous yell. The wagon door opened. A grizzly, bearded man peered into the night, a hand shielding his eyes from the storm. When he made me out, he shouted, "Com en, frien."

He was a Basque and couldn't speak much more English than that. That was okay. I didn't need conversation, I needed warmth and food, and the Basque shepherd had plenty of both. A little stove heated the little wagon. On the stovetop, coffee perked and beans fried in a skillet. The Basque handed me a tin plate and cup and then filled them.

I ate heartily, and the shepherd resumed his music, serenading me with guitar and lyrics in a tongue I didn't know. Anyhow, I heard a clear message in this music. As I sat there warm and fed and restored, I knew this music said, Never give up hope! The Lord'll give you shelter even when you think none is near.

Soon I was back in the saddle, strong enough to ward off the storm. I caught up with my horses and was home by noon.

By and by these days—when I get to feeling pitiful about my failing eyes, when I'm inclined to think there's little hope for this old fellow—I need to remind myself of that music in the midst of a storm. The music of a shepherd that convinced me that the Lord is always my shepherd. I won't give up hope.

2 LOVE . . . GOD'S ETERNAL GIFT TO US

And now these three remain: faith, hope and love.
But the greatest of these is love.

—1 Corinthians 13:13

LOVE AT ANY AGE by John Martin Mason

Ten-year-old Susie came running into my rectory office. Her eyes were bright, her blonde hair was windblown, and she had exciting news to share.

"I have a boyfriend!" she exclaimed.

"You do?" I replied. "Tell me about him."

"Well, he's pretty quiet. But he's the cutest boy in our class. And he's been my boyfriend now for a day and a half!"

I congratulated her and then excused myself. One of our seventy-year-old women parishioners had called, asking me to come over to her home. She ushered me in, but before I could sit down, she burst out her news.

"Guess what? I have a gentleman friend! We've been going together for six months now. And it just keeps getting better. Why, he's the handsomest man you ever saw!"

She went on and on, picturing his virtues. And as I listened, I realized that the capacity to love is the one human function unimpaired by aging. Eyesight dims, hearing fails, bones grow brittle, memory lapses. But our ability to love—and be loved—remains unchanged. It's God's eternal gift to us.

BECOMING REAL by Sue Monk Kidd

Last year, I sat beneath a funeral awning in the warm Georgia sun and watched as my grandmother was buried. While the minister spoke, I remembered the last time I had seen her. She'd held my seven-year-old daughter in her lap, and as Ann moved her finger along the folds of Grandma's face, Grandma said, "Those are my wrinkles. They mean I'm getting very old."

Later Ann asked me if wrinkles hurt. But it seemed to me she was really asking about what it meant to grow old. To answer her, I pulled Margery Williams' classic, *The Velveteen Rabbit*, from the shelf and read it to her.

It was the story of a new toy rabbit that came to live in a little boy's nursery. More than anything, the Rabbit yearned to know the secret of becoming "real." One day he asked the Skin Horse, who was so old his brown coat was rubbing off, how to become REAL. "Real isn't how you are made," he told the Rabbit. "It's a thing that happens to you. When a child loves you for a long, long time...then you become Real." The Rabbit then asked, "Does it hurt?"

"Sometimes," he answered.... "Generally, by the time you are Real, most of your hair has been loved off, and your eyes drop out and you get loose in the joints and very shabby. But these things don't matter at all, because once you are Real you can't be ugly, except to people who don't understand."

When I finished reading I said, "You see, Ann, Grandma Monk is just getting 'real.' That's all." And there was a wonderful light in Ann's eyes....

As the memory faded, I sat on the cemetery hill and thought about the children, grandchildren, and great-grandchildren who had sat on Grandma's lap, wearing it nearly away. I remembered all the joint-loosening miles I had dragged her through the park... the afternoon I brought my baby chick into her lace-curtained parlor, poured oatmeal on the rug for him, and saw Grandma's eyes nearly drop out...the time I was learning to drive and carried her on a wild ride through the yard, narrowly missing a pine tree. More white hairs. Another wrinkle. The Skin Horse was right. It can be wearing to be loved by a child.

The service ended. Now I stood among the people beside her grave, thinking about birth and death and the journey in between. And I knew something clearly, more clearly than I'd known it before. We become authentic persons through our willingness to love and be loved—even when it means becoming worn by sacrifice, even when the demands make our faces wrinkle and our joints grow loose.

Driving away, I caught the reflection of my face in the car window. It reminded me of the fine lines gathering around my own eyes and the hints of gray slipping into my hair. But I wouldn't think of these aging signs quite the same anymore. For growing old could be a wondrous passage. And the markings of it didn't matter, except to those who didn't understand. What mattered was becoming "real." What mattered was loving and being loved for a long, long time.

WIDOW AND WIDOWER by Marjorie Holmes
and George Schmieler

Marjorie: On the evening of January 1, I sat at my desk, anticipating the new year ahead. It had been thirteen months since my husband, Lynn, died. We'd been married forty-seven years, and I'd missed him and mourned him. But he'd been desperately sick with cancer, and neither I nor our four children had wanted his torment extended by even a single day.

Now, after a year, I felt at peace about Lynn—and myself. God had blessed me with wonderful health. At the age of seventy, I still swam, danced, and water-skied. I still had many things to write. And I'd even begun to wonder if there might not be another person to share this good life with. *In the new year,* I thought, *perhaps...*

George: On the evening of January 1, I sat in the bedroom my late wife, Carolyn, and I had shared. I was alone and bitter. In the months since her death, I'd been withdrawn, in retreat from my three children and my friends, losing weight, dying inside myself. Carolyn and I had had forty-eight beautiful, ardent years, but now marriage was lost to me forever. I was too broken. It was too late.

Marjorie: During the year just ended, even my children had encouraged me to think about finding companionship. "Pray for someone special," my daughter, Melanie, had advised.

Why not? Lately, each morning after my shower and each night at bedtime, I'd begun to pray, "Please, God, send me a wonderful man who will love me and whom I can love." I wasn't in any hurry; I just felt if this were God's will, it would happen. Now I took a sheet of paper from my desk drawer and, half whimsically, I wrote down the qualifications I would desire in a potential husband:

1. A believer, devout. 2. Good health. 3. Successful professionally. 4. Intelligent, well read. 5. Good talker, good listener. 6. Sexy, ardent. 7. Good dancer. (Not absolutely essential, but why not ask for what you want?)

George: When Carolyn died, very suddenly, my whole world collapsed. I was like a child turned out in a strange city in the dark. I didn't know what to do. Carolyn had been not only my sweetheart and companion but also secretary, bookkeeper, and nurse for my medical practice. She handled everything. I never wrote a check or paid a bill. I didn't even answer the telephone.

From the day of her death, I was like a zombie—a man literally ill, almost autistic, with grief. To keep my sanity, I continued to see patients, but my zest for life was completely gone. I wouldn't even accept a dinner invitation from friends, let alone consider marrying again. It was unthinkable.

Now, sitting in our bedroom on New Year's night, I heard my voice cursing God.

Marjorie: The new year was six weeks old when my phone rang on a bright February morning and I heard a stranger's voice saying, "I love you. You saved my life." I listened. As a writer, you learn to listen, sometimes puzzled, always expectant, never shocked. You learn to recognize those whose need is real. This was no kook. The voice, as it went on, told me he was a doctor from suburban Pittsburgh who'd been absolutely devastated by the loss of his wife. Though his family, friends, and patients had tried desperately, he'd been inconsolable—lonely, wild with grief, suicidal. Then, on New Year's night he'd come across my book, *I've Got to Talk to Somebody, God*. Under quite amazing circumstances.

George: Exactly at the moment I cursed God, a picture of me that had been on Carolyn's dresser pitched forward and crashed to the floor. No wind, no bolt of lightning, just an abrupt crash. Shaken, I dropped to my knees. "God, forgive me. But help me, help me."

I raised my head and found myself staring at the door of a closet beside the bed, noticing for the first time that its panels formed a cross. Something urged me to open the door and to reach right down under a pile of Carolyn's things—dresses, purses, knitting materials, what have you. And what my fingers found and brought out was, of all improbable things, a book, a book called *I've Got to Talk to Somebody, God,* by Marjorie Holmes.

Reading it helped. It told me that the author had suffered, that a lot of people suffer, but with the help of God, they can and must go on. I read it over and over.

I knew that somehow, if only to please my worried family, I had to try to come out of my personal tomb. Finally, I decided to accept the invitation of a Florida couple who'd been very close to Carolyn and me. They'd been begging me to visit—and on the drive south, I could visit my son, Jeff.

When I got to Silver Spring, Maryland, where Jeff lives, I opened my suitcase and there on top of my clothes was *I've Got to Talk to Somebody, God*. I didn't even remember packing it! Staring at it, I read the information on the jacket for the first time.

The author lived not far away, somewhere in the Washington, DC, area. I'd never before as much as written to an author, let alone tried to contact one in person. But now I knew I had to try to contact this one, this Marjorie Holmes.

Hours and innumerable phone calls later, I got through to a pleasant man who said, "Why, yes, her husband was my cousin— he died about a year ago. Yes, I'll give you her number."

Marjorie: The man on the phone went on to tell me that after God had put my book in his hands, it had literally pursued him on this trip to Florida. He felt he had to call me.

"Somehow, I knew you'd been widowed before I heard about it," he added. "If you're still free, may I come to see you?"

"Yes, I'm free," I said, pleased and touched. "But unfortunately I'm just leaving on a two-week speaking trip."

"I'll stay on with my son till you come back," he insisted. And, unlikely as it seemed at the time, he did.

When I returned, the mailbox was stuffed with notes postmarked Silver Spring. And when I called, simply because I'd promised, he whooped for joy. "Will you have dinner with me tomorrow night?"

The next evening a handsome, six-foot man walked in the door, his arms full of roses. On the way to the restaurant he sang to me in the most beautiful male voice I've ever heard. He was poised and gallant and funny and for real. He had brought along his little black doctor's bag full of pictures, clippings, and "credentials." We talked for hours. And when he kissed me, it seemed perfectly in order. But when he asked me to marry him, I said no, firmly but gently. "Not because 'this is so sudden.' Because you're still in love with your wife, George. And from all the things you've told me, I know I never could be the kind of wife she was to you."

George: Mere weeks ago, I'd found the idea of remarrying unthinkable. Now I was begging for the hand of a woman I'd met in person only a few hours earlier. And I'd never felt more sure of myself in my life.

"But I love you now!" I told Marjorie when she rejected my proposal. "The past is gone, it's all over. Something happened the minute I heard your voice. It was like waking up from a nightmare. And when I actually saw you. It's not your book, it's you, the wonderful time we've had together just in these past few hours. We need each other. God Himself must have brought us together. Please say you'll at least make an effort to get to know me."

Patiently she explained just how difficult that would be. "You're practicing in Pittsburgh, and I'm researching a new book and still winding up promotion commitments on the last one. I'm really not right for you, George. A large part of me will always be married to my career."

"But at least you'll let me drive over to see you again."

"I'm sorry. I'm packing for a trip to Israel. Maybe when I get back."

I took her home docilely, but I didn't take no for an answer. Marjorie relented and let me visit—and see her off for Israel. When she came back, three weeks later, I was waiting at the airport with an armload of flowers. I bombarded her with letters, phone calls, gifts, more flowers. Then I persuaded her to spend the week before Easter with me, visiting my son Jeff's vacation home in Ocean City, Maryland.

It was a marvelous, carefree week of running the dogs on the beach, swimming, dancing. Never had I enjoyed anyone's company so much. And the most wonderful part: Marjorie seemed to take an equal pleasure in me. On Easter Sunday, as we knelt together in church, I worked up the courage to try again. Squeezing her hand, I asked the crucial question.

Marjorie: "Yes, oh yes!" I whispered. Never mind that here was a man who would never get over his wife (I thought). Never mind that I couldn't balance a checkbook, let alone fill the multiple roles that Carolyn had filled for him. What really mattered was that God had sent me "a wonderful man who loved me and whom I could love." And did!

We rushed home from church and called our families. They were thrilled. Eventually we chose the Fourth of July for our wedding day and planned an outdoor, lakeside ceremony.

It rained torrents that day. But the sun broke through just an hour before the appointed time. People mopped off the chairs, the minister arrived, the music began to play. I wore a pink dress the color of the sunset. And as George and I joined hands to repeat our vows, the most beautiful rainbow I've ever seen arched the sky.

When we returned from our honeymoon and I was packing up books and papers for the move to Pittsburgh, I came across the forgotten list of qualifications I'd written for my future husband. "George, you won't believe this," I told him, and read them out loud.

"Who is this guy?" he grinned. Then, taking the list to look for himself, he exclaimed. "You mean you wrote this on January first?"

I nodded.

"About what time?"

"Around ten at night, as I recall. Why do you ask?"

"That's when it happened! When the picture fell! When I was in such terrible despair until something told me to reach into the closet and I found your book!"

The picture falling. The book turning up in his closet and later in his suitcase. His son living in the vicinity of my home. His tracing a number that proved to be that of Lynn's cousin. I remember reading somewhere, "There are no coincidences, only Godincidences."

George: Since our marriage, I've continued to see patients and Marjorie has continued to write. We're both convinced that the best way to live a vital, enthusiastic life is to keep doing the work that satisfies you. As for love, I think it's like a savings account. It draws interest and builds. If your first marriage was rich in love, that means you have an even greater store of love to lavish on the second.

Marjorie: I agree with George about love generating more love. Even so, I must try to answer an important question.

Is it possible to take the place of a mate who has been loved so long?

No.

That place will be separate and sacred forever. What the second husband or wife must realize is that a new place has been created.

And the second love is no less thrilling, beautiful, or enduring simply because this new door to the heart has been opened later. As George says, the richer and finer the love that has gone before, the greater this second love can be.

And truly, our life together grows sweeter with every year.

SHOWING MY AGE by Julia Attaway

I slid into a pew on the side aisle, checked on baby Stephen sleeping in the stroller, and looked around. The church wasn't crowded, but a goodly number of people were there for the funeral. Most of them I recognized.

I hadn't been back to the church where Andrew and I met and married since we'd moved away eight years ago. The nineteenth-century building still looked to be in pretty good shape. I was kind of surprised, though, at how much older the people seemed. It actually took me a few moments to identify a couple of them.

Stephen murmured that he was awake, so I unbuckled him and picked him up. When I looked around again a few moments later, I saw that people had noted my presence too. Much to my surprise, I could see mild puzzlement on a few faces. It was almost as if they didn't quite recognize me.

Did I look older too?

I added up the signs of my aging. I have some wisps of gray now. ("Don't complain," Andrew chides me. "At least you have hair!") My skin isn't quite as taut as it used to be. I think I look my age.

Even though the mirror had been hinting at this transformation for some time, it was disconcerting to see my aging confirmed in the eyes of others. I looked down at Stephen as if to ask what he thought. He gurgled and smiled and made a grab for my streak of gray. I smiled back. Stephen couldn't care less how many wrinkles I had, as long as they creased into smiles of love. That seemed to be a good way to look at it.

WHEN GOD REACHES OUT THROUGH OTHER PEOPLE by Elizabeth Sherrill

The dinner party brought together various branches of the family. The seats of honor at the ends of the long table went to the two eldest: my grandfather, Papa—then in his mideighties—and Grammy, my brother-in-law's grandmother—age ninety-four.

Isolated by deafness, Papa had become almost morbidly interested in the details of illness, both his own and other people's. The table was buzzing with lively conversations when he shouted to Grammy, above the chattering voices, "How's your heart?"

Grammy beamed down the long table at him, a beatific smile that encompassed the entire gathering and seemed to take in all of struggling humanity as well. She answered his question with a single word, "Enlarged."

Papa did not hear, and "enlarged" was relayed to him along the seats. Sitting beside him, I shrieked into his ear, "Her heart's enlarged."

Medically, of course, a serious condition. But as I said the words, I thought they also summed up God's will for all of us as our years increase. Grammy's answer has become for me a kind of shorthand prayer. *Like Grammy, let me carry my aches and ailments lightly as I grow older! Each year, let me care a little less about myself, a little more for others.*

NEVER TOO LATE FOR LOVE by Ruth L. Wolfgang

Lingering at the doorway of my apartment in the retirement complex, Frank Wolfgang took my hand in his. "Ruth," he said, his voice catching a little, "I'd like to ask you something."

My heart skipped a beat. I sensed what his question would be, but for the life of me, I didn't know how I would answer.

"Ruth," he went on, "would you consider...marrying me?"

Flustered, I hesitated, not wanting to hurt him, yet determined to be honest. "I don't know, I just don't know," I said. At the age of seventy-seven and never married, I enjoyed being retired and going where I wanted whenever I pleased. I looked into Frank's penetrating blue eyes and felt the enormity of my decision. "I've been on my own for such a long while, Frank. I need some time to think this through."

"I can wait," he said.

That night I tossed and turned. Marriage? To Frank Wolfgang? It wasn't as though he was a stranger. We had known each other for more than fifty years. His wife, Naomi, had been my roommate in college and a great friend ever since. After her death, Frank and I had mourned our loss together. As time went by, we had become even closer. But I wondered, *What would Naomi think?*

We had been schoolgirls when we met at Millersville State Teachers College, outside of Lancaster, Pennsylvania. I had grown up on a farm, and I arrived at the dormitory with all my belongings in a single brown suitcase. She was sitting on her bed in what would be our room. "Hi, I'm Ruth Long," I said, extending my hand.

"I'm Naomi Hoch," she said, smiling. We both burst out laughing. Just like Ruth and Naomi in the Bible. I felt we were destined to be friends.

Naomi was in a circle of girls who could afford to ride the trolley into town on Saturday afternoons and end up at Hupper's Confectionery for a sundae. My friends and I saved our pennies by taking long walks in the country. But I soon learned that beneath her sophisticated veneer, Naomi was a down-to-earth, loyal friend. When she married Frank, I couldn't have been happier for her.

I remember how impressed with Frank I was when I visited their apartment. Frank excused himself to the kitchen so we could enjoy each other's company. "You always cook," he said to Naomi. "This time, leave it to me."

Back home, I told my mother, "If I ever meet a man like Frank Wolfgang, you'll never have to worry about my being single."

In the years after college, I was busy teaching during the day and working on my master's degree on weekends. There were a couple of young men who came into my life, but in the end, there always turned out to be something that wasn't right.

The oldest of five children, I returned to the farm to care for my father when he took sick, and after his death I cared for my mother. A few years short of retirement, I stopped teaching altogether because of family obligations. Only after Mother's death did I take another job, at a missionary school in Japan.

All the while, I kept up with Frank and Naomi. Whenever Naomi needed a substitute for her bridge group, she called me and I spent the night. Several times I went on trips with them, as a fourth with Naomi's sister. When I settled in the retirement community, I looked forward to many more years of friendship. But now there was only Frank and me.

He's just looking for someone to take care of him, I tried to tell myself, abandoning all hope of sleep. But then I stopped to consider how good he was at taking care of himself. *He's lonely and looking for companionship,* I told myself. But he had plenty of interests—gourmet cooking, classical music, books—and didn't seem dependent on a wife for entertainment. Then I considered how much I enjoyed his companionship.

Our courtship had really taken off when we went on a picnic one Sunday afternoon. I had packed a basket with sandwiches, potato salad, and Japanese spinach rolls, and we drove to a quiet spot near the Conestoga River. We spread out a checkered tablecloth and sat down for our feast.

"Ruth, these spinach rolls are fantastic," Frank exclaimed, the early-September sun glistening on his white hair. He wiped his mouth and then cleared his throat. "I guess you know I've been coming to see you because I enjoy being with you."

After our meal, we packed the picnic basket and put it in the car. The next thing I knew, I felt Frank's warm, strong hand take hold of mine. We walked along the grassy riverbank for some time, talking about all the things we had in common. Then, when he dropped me off at my apartment, he kissed me.

The memory of that kiss still fresh, I paced my bedroom, trying to decide what to do about his proposal. I still kept thinking of Naomi. What would my dear friend have said?

The answer finally occurred to me: She would have wished me the very best. That's what friends do. I prayed, "Lord, I believe this is what You want. Bless us in our marriage."

In the ensuing days, there was a flurry of excitement caused by Frank's and my announcement. Women friends stopped by to admire my ruby engagement ring. When I called my former pastor, I asked him, "Would you be able to perform a wedding in a few months?"

"Whose?" he asked.

"Mine."

There was dead silence and then joyous laughter.

Saturday, November 7, I stood in the hallway outside the chapel, dressed in rose-colored chiffon. More nervous than I had ever been before, I relaxed when Frank came down the hall, looking sharp in his gray, pinstriped suit. The two of us took our cue from the organ and walked arm in arm down the aisle.

That evening, Frank and I sat across from each other at a romantic, candlelit table on the first night of our honeymoon. The waitress admired my orchid corsage. "Celebrating?" she asked.

"Yes, indeed," I said.

When we ordered, we ended up asking for the same thing, down to the salad dressing. "Have you two always agreed on everything like this?" the waitress asked.

Frank winked at me and grinned. "Why, yes, all of our married life!"

We moved into my apartment, and this November we'll celebrate our eleventh anniversary. We've had a few physical ups and downs, and we don't travel too far anymore, but every day we count our blessings.

Sometimes God saves the best for last.

GRANDMA AND THE PAPER GIRL by Ella Duquette

I squinted against the afternoon sunshine, looking out the window for the paperboy. Ever since a stroke had weakened my legs, I hadn't been able to get around so well. I depended on the paper to keep me up-to-date with a world from which I often felt disconnected. When the paper came late, I got edgy. Finally I saw someone coming down the street. A girl, no more than ten or eleven years old, hurled a rolled-up newspaper toward my screen door. It landed with a thud.

"Just a minute," I called out the window. "Where's the usual carrier?"

"I'm the carrier now, lady," she said, hands on her hips.

"Well, the old one used to bring the paper in to me."

"Oh yeah? Well, I can do that." She came in and plopped the paper onto my lap, and I got a better look at her. Frayed shorts and a cropped top—and it wasn't even summer yet. She tossed back her shoulder-length red hair and blew a huge pink bubble.

"I hate bubble gum," I said.

"Tough beans," she said.

I gasped. This snippy little thing needed to be taught some manners.

"The children around here call me Mrs. Lee, after my late husband."

"Well, you can call me Kristin," she said with a sassy tilt of her head and then bounded down the steps.

Just what I need, I thought. Nothing was easy anymore. Simple tasks like dusting and doing laundry were an ordeal these days. And baking, which I used to love, was far too much trouble. My husband, Lee, and most of my friends had passed on. Lately I had found myself wondering why the Lord had left me behind. It was clear to me, anyway, that if young people today all acted like that smart-alecky papergirl, I had been too long in this world.

Kristin's attitude didn't much improve over the following weeks. But I had to admit she never missed a day or forgot to bring the paper inside to me. She even took to sharing some small talk when she stopped by. She came in from a wicked rainstorm once and pulled the paper out from under her coat.

"H—of a day, huh, Gram?" she said, handing me the paper.

I could feel the muscles in my jaw tense. "Do you talk like that just to shock me?" I asked. "And I'm not your grandmother."

"I just talk like all my friends."

"Not in this house, you don't," I shot back. "In my day, you'd have your mouth washed out with soap."

She laughed. "You'd have some fight on your hands if you tried it, Gram," she retorted.

I threw up my hands. *Why do I even bother with you?* I wondered, as she strutted down the street.

But she started coming by after her paper route and other times as well, chitchatting happily about school, her friends. Each time she left, it was as if a radio had been turned off. One day, a bundle of newspapers slipped from her hands onto the floor and she uttered a dirty word. Instantly she clapped a hand over her mouth and said, "Oops! Sorry, Gram."

Well, she's learned something, I thought, smiling secretly.

I dug out some of my old photographs and outfits, thinking she might like to see them. She never tired of my stories of growing up on a farm—how we had raised our own food and washed our clothes by hand. *All this girl needs is someone to fuss over her,* I thought. *Why else would she keep coming back when I'm always fussing at her over her clothes or talk? God, is that why You're keeping me around—for Kristin?*

She showed me her report card when I asked one afternoon.

"This is awful," I said.

"I do better than lots of kids," she snapped.

"You're not 'lots of kids.' Have a little pride in yourself."

"Oh, Gram, you make such a big deal out of things," she said. But I kept after her about her grades.

A short time later, Kristin gave up her paper route and shifted her visits to after school. I didn't ask why she kept coming to see me because—though I wouldn't have been caught dead admitting it—her visits had become the highlight of my days.

Once she told me, giggling, about some of her friends who had been shoplifting.

"That's nothing to laugh about, young lady," I said. "It's stealing, plain and simple."

"Well, I didn't do it."

"All the same, you could be guilty by association. Your reputation goes with you all your life, you know."

"Oh, Gram, stop preaching."

"If you don't like it, there's the door," I declared. But she didn't leave. In fact, we spent more time together. Still, we had our moments. Like when she baked a cake and then sank down on a chair without laying a finger to the mound of dishes.

"Come back here and clean up after yourself," I ordered.

"No way. I'm not putting my hands in that sink. It's gross." She had just polished her nails—a ghastly purple.

"Tough beans!" I blurted. She laughed. *Mercy,* I thought, *now I'm starting to talk like her.* But she did the dishes that day and many another. I taught her how to bake fresh bread and my famous apple pie. It was wonderful to smell those familiar smells coming from the kitchen again. One Sunday, Kristin stopped by. "You didn't go to church dressed like that, did you?" I asked.

She glanced at her shorts and T-shirt. "All the kids dress like this."

"I've told you before, Kristin, you're not 'all the kids.'"

"Well, I suppose you think I should wear one of your old outfits, complete with hat and long, white gloves!" She flounced out the door, only to come back a moment later. "I'm sorry, Gram," she said, giving me a quick hug. "Forgive me?"

How could I not? Making up with her seemed as natural as making up with one of my own daughters after a fight. Gradually, Kristin started dusting and cleaning up around the house, without the slightest hint from me. She even did my laundry. It chafed at my pride to let her do things I had done for myself all my life—but she was insistent. And this was the same girl who just a short while earlier wouldn't put her hands into a sink of dirty dishes!

"How about I set your hair?" she asked one day. "My mom taught me."

This was too much. "I'm not so old and helpless that I can't take care of myself."

"Oh, don't be so stubborn. Come on, Gram," she wheedled. For the first time, that nickname didn't annoy me. I gave in, and she proceeded to work several different lathery formulas into my short locks, not letting me look in a mirror until she was done. I had visions of my hair dyed the same awful purple as her fingernails. I was amazed to find it soft, shiny, and still blonde.

"You're good at this," I said, and Kristin beamed.

I was even more impressed when, shortly after graduating from eighth grade, Kristin brought me a scrapbook filled with certificates of academic achievement.

"See? I told you that you weren't like everybody," I said, hugging her. "You're special." It was wonderful to see she valued my approval. But the best part was seeing that she was pleased with herself.

I still didn't think much of her study habits. She insisted on keeping the television on when she did homework. I couldn't fathom how she could concentrate with that racket. But then, there was a lot I couldn't fathom about Kristin's world. "Gram, do you know there are eight girls pregnant in the freshman class?" she told me. I gasped. "And that's nothing," she continued. "In some schools, they have police guards and metal detectors and just about everybody smokes, drinks, and takes drugs."

I shuddered. *It's so different nowadays, Lord. How can I help her deal with all these things I know nothing about?* Then I thought of how far Kristin had already come, and I knew the best thing I could do was to keep being there for her, as she always was for me.

One evening recently, she brought over a cake mix. "I'm going to bake us a superduper double-chocolate cake, Gram," she announced.

"No way," I said. "Shortcuts won't make a cake as good as from scratch."

"Oh, come on, Gram. It's easier this way."

"Don't 'Oh, Gram' me, young lady. Easier isn't always better, and in this house—" She broke into laughter—the laughter I had come to know so well—and in a moment, I joined in.

Kristin shook her head and took my hand. "I don't know what it is, Gram," she said. "We hardly ever agree on anything, and you make me so mad sometimes. But I always come back. I guess I must love you."

Who would have known that when I looked out the window for the paper carrier that afternoon five years ago, I would end up finding my best friend?

3 PEACE . . . THROUGH PRAYER

Do not be anxious about anything,
but in everything by prayer and supplication
with thanksgiving let your requests be made known to God.
And the peace of God, which surpasses all understanding,
will guard your hearts and your minds in Christ Jesus.

—Philippians 4:6—7 (esv)

A TIME TO EVERY PURPOSE
by Marilyn Morgan King

Koheleth—the Teacher—and author of Ecclesiastes, writes that there's "a time to every purpose under the heaven." And I ask myself, *So why do I so often feel as if I'm running a race against time—and losing?* As I hold this question in prayer, I see that the deeper question is *How am I using the hours, minutes, and seconds I have left? Am I making time for . . .*

rocking another newborn grandchild
in these aging arms,
so well practiced in baby-rocking;
breathing in pink and coral sunsets,
white satin moons, and
silent mountains
that take away my breath;
the simple things:
fixing a soup-and-fruit supper,
watering the plants,
sweeping the kitchen floor?

Saying "I love you"
to my husband, children, and grandchildren;
"Good-bye" to old friends;
"Thank you" to mentors;
"I'm coming" to the
Mystery I call Beloved?

And the answer comes: How much time? Only this God-given moment—only this eternal now.

A NEW ME by Jay Earle

"Your tests show you have rheumatoid arthritis, Jay," my doctor said. Arthritis? Wasn't that what everyone my age had a touch of? Besides, I felt so great that day, it never dawned on me that I might have a serious problem.

Two weeks earlier I'd been to him when my knee stiffened up—the result, I assumed, of a sixty-seven-year-old guy taking one too many runs on the slalom course waterskiing. I headed to the doctor so he could "fix it." And fix it he did. The cortisone shot worked its magic, and my knee felt as good as new. Sure, I suffered the usual aches and pains of getting older, but it wasn't anything I couldn't handle.

Now—two weeks later—I drove home and spent the afternoon spreading mulch and spiffing up my boat. I didn't give my diagnosis another thought. And yet, as the shot wore off over the following weeks, it became impossible to ignore the symptoms. At first it was just hard to get up off the ground after playing with my grandkids. Then I started to have trouble standing at my work-bench while using a saw or drill. What was happening to my body?

I'd always thought of physical pain as a temporary condition, something I could tough out or work through. Only if it got really bad would I see a doctor. But this rheumatoid arthritis was unlike anything I'd ever experienced. The pain was constant and everywhere, and instead of getting better, it got worse. I couldn't sleep, I couldn't read, I could barely even watch TV. Waterskiing? Hiking? Forget about it. Overnight, I'd become an old man.

My doctor sent me to a rheumatologist. He tried me on a variety of medications. "It may take some trial and error to find the right combination," he warned.

I'm not the most patient guy. While I waited in vain for relief, I wanted to scream, *Don't you people understand? I'm Jay Earle. I'm not some cranky old man who hobbles around complaining about how he feels.* Everything I'd ever done had come through determination and hard work—swabbing decks in the Navy, putting myself through college by playing saxophone in a dance band, working harder than the next guy in my banking career. I had always counted on my own strength, so now when friends said that they were praying for me, I said thanks, but didn't put much stock in it. Never had, really. All I wanted was the old me back.

One morning, I snapped at my wife over nothing, an all too common occurrence since my diagnosis. I retreated to my work-shop and picked up my power drill. I made a few holes in a nice piece of hardwood. All at once my hands failed me. The drill slipped, gouging the wood. In a blind rage, I slammed the drill to the ground. For about a minute I felt better. Then the adrenaline subsided. There I was with a useless aching body and a broken drill.

That night, I couldn't sleep. I couldn't even get out of bed and go downstairs and try to watch some TV. I was alone in the dark with my pain, a pain that had become the largest presence in my life. My mind jumped from thought to thought, trying to outrun it. Yet the pain invaded everything. I found myself thinking about the prayer list my wife had put me on at her church. Prayer had always struck me as a pretty passive approach to solving problems. But now my mind flashed back to other people I'd known with chronic conditions—friends who'd been hurt in terrible car accidents, family members who'd fought cancer. So much suffering, yet people survived, even prevailed over pain. All of them had faith. Was it the hand of God that supported them? Was it the power of prayer and the thankfulness that people felt for His blessings?

Yes, I'd been lucky. Great jobs. A wonderful family. My patient, loving wife. My house by the lake. I had always assumed that most of it came by way of brains and some tough decision-making. Hard work. But maybe . . . maybe it was because God was looking out for me. Maybe He would look out for me now. "Lord," I whispered in the dark, "I turn to You. If I must have this pain, help me to bear it." Soon I fell back to sleep.

The doctor kept juggling my meds until gradually there was improvement. "I think we've hit on the right combination," he said. I couldn't ski anymore, but I could spend the day boating with hardly any pain. The joints in my hands improved so much I picked up the saxophone again. I'd forgotten what a pleasure it was to play music. The doctor might have found the right combination of drugs, but I had found another powerful combination—faith and gratitude.

Arthritis is part of my life these days, but it doesn't control it. For that, I am boundlessly grateful. I did something I should have done years ago. I joined my wife's church. Now I not only have a congregation of people praying for me, but I have a list of people I'm saying prayers for. I work just as hard on it as any of the jobs I've ever done. And I visit the sick in the hospital. It helps me to help them.

Physically, I'd say I'm back to 90 percent of where I was before the arthritis hit. But spiritually, I'm a different person. And you know what? At my age, that's pretty exciting. I don't have the old me back. I've got something new, something I'd needed for a long time.

I'M TOO YOUNG FOR THIS by Karen Barber

The woman on the phone said she was a nurse. "Ms. Barber, I'm calling from your HMO. I just wanted to let you know we're writing a prescription for you—it's a bone-restoration medication. Your scan results show that you have osteoporosis."

Clunk. I dropped my laundry basket, heavy with one more load before our vacation to Colorado. "Osteoporosis?" I sputtered. She must have the wrong Karen Barber. No way could I have osteoporosis! I was young—well, not old, anyway—the picture of health.

The nurse, apparently unaware that this was the first I'd heard the news, launched into an explanation of how to take the pills. "In the morning, on an empty stomach..." Her voice faded in my mind. *Osteoporosis?* Yes, I'd had a bone-density scan a month before, but only because my general practitioner had insisted—something about standard procedure after menopause. But osteoporosis? That was an old person's disease, right? I power walked two and a half miles each day! The only reason I'd even been in the doctor's office was to get checked out for an upcoming mission trip to Honduras. Frail, old people did not take mission trips to Honduras. Surely there was a mistake.

The nurse, however, referred to the exact date I'd had my scan. She asked if I had any questions. Too stunned to think, I mumbled no and hung up. I stared at the laundry, piled high in the basket. Every year my husband, Gordon, our three boys, and our daughter-in-law spent a week at a cabin in the Colorado mountains. Everyone else skied—I didn't know how—while I took long walks on the mountain roads. What did this mean, osteoporosis? That I was too frail for trips like that? Come on, I was only fifty-four. Gordon and I had so many plans now that our youngest was about to leave for college. I exercised every morning—walking and praying—drank plenty of milk, ate yogurt, took calcium supplements. I hadn't broken a bone since I was five years old. *Not fair, God. I'm too young for this!*

A few days later, we left for Colorado. I didn't fill the prescription and barely mentioned the nurse's call to Gordon. No sense worrying him, especially if this all turned out to be a big mistake. Besides, the nurse had said something about stomach upset as a possible side effect. I certainly didn't want that on vacation. I tried to put the whole thing out of my mind.

At the cabin, though, I found myself feeling irrationally fearful. I had toyed with the idea of taking skiing lessons and joining the others on the slopes. What if I fell? Would my bones snap? Well, I could at least try some sledding. I looked at my boots by the door. Fear surged again, and for a moment, the entire outdoors loomed like an endless danger zone—a world of potential falls and broken bones. I flopped down on the sofa and turned on the TV. A single phone call had accomplished what fifty-four years of life had not. Suddenly I felt old.

Well, I thought when we got back home, *I'm not dealing with this now.* Each day, I found a new excuse not to go to the pharmacy. When I ran out of excuses, I decided to confront my doctor. I would tell him about my healthy, active lifestyle, and he would say, "Of course, Ms. Barber, you don't need medication. There must have been some mistake."

The doctor listened and then fixed me with a patient but pointed look. "Ms. Barber, there's no other way to put it. You have osteoporosis." He drew a picture: two circles, one filled with dense, crosshatched lines, the other with just a few lines. "These are normal bones," he said, pointing to the full circle. "Lots of bone mass here, which in a young woman's body is constantly being replenished. After menopause, though, estrogen levels go down and the body stops replacing bone mass so reliably." He tapped the other circle.

"But, I'm young!" I protested. "I take calcium pills."

"Osteoporosis affects women of *all* ages," he replied, "even some men. And the fact is, people who have it need supplementation to help their bodies absorb calcium. Often, you can't replace bone mass you've lost. But you can keep what remains—if you take the medication."

Dejected, I dragged myself to the pharmacy. The crowning insult came with the pharmacist's instructions. I would have to take the pill first thing in the morning on an empty stomach and then eat nothing and remain upright for half an hour. What did that mean? No breakfast? Could I still take my walks? I was becoming an old lady tethered to her pills!

The next morning, I woke up and looked in the medicine cabinet. The orange pill bottle stared back at me. I had spent the previous evening poring over the instruction sheet and looking up the medication online. Lots of unpleasant side effects, especially the stomach upset. I had a meeting at church. *Best not to risk feeling sick. I'll start tomorrow*, I thought, and closed the cabinet.

The next day was the same, and the day after that. Always some reason to postpone. The pills greeted me each morning, silent ambassadors from the land of old age. I'd stare at them, waver, and close the cabinet.

One misty spring morning, I left the house for my six o'clock walk. I liked to pray on these walks, a different kind of prayer on each section. I glided through our woodsy backyard, smelling the damp earth. I crossed a bridge over a creek and climbed a hill past some tennis courts to the road. The road was where I switched to thankfulness prayers—not asking God for anything, just thanking Him for what I already had and the blessings I knew I would continue to receive. I thanked Him for

Gordon, for the boys, our house, the beautiful morning. And, suddenly, without quite realizing it, I found myself thanking Him for those osteoporosis pills. The pills?! Yes, the pills. My prayer rolled on. *Thank You, God, for my doctor who watches over me so wisely. For the scan machine that found this problem with my bones. And for supplying a way to fix it. You take such good care of me.*

The mist was lifting, the sun beginning to illuminate the road with soft, daffodil-colored light. I felt a warmth inside of me too, some small but profound shift. All this time, I had been regarding these pills as my enemy—an unfair, unwanted sign of advancing age, of mortality, of lost youth. But that's not what they were at all. They were a gift, a life-giving gift. I didn't need to fear them. I knew I should be grateful for them. Indeed, just thinking of them that way—as something to be thankful for—drove out my fear.

I wasn't afraid of the pills, I realized. I was afraid of growing old. I was in denial of the most basic plan God had laid out for us, of a journey that began and ended with Him.

The mist disappeared and the sun shone on me brightly. I finished the walk, entered the house, and made straight for the medicine cabinet.

Today, nearly a year later, I take my medication regularly and have suffered not a single side effect. Gordon and I recently got back from a European cruise—our empty-nester dividend.

Am I old? I think about that question differently now. God knows the number of my years. And He's giving me what I need to make the most of them. Just like He always has.

"WE PRAYED FOR YOU" by Kathleen Kinderfather

I looked up at the snow-crowned peak of the Mount of the Holy Cross, stark and eerie in the light of dawn. The roughly five-mile zigzag trek from our base camp at 10,300 feet to the 14,005-foot summit included a special obstacle: a massive field of boulders, some of them taller than my five-foot frame. For a week my climbing partner, Jody, and I had hiked the mountains of Colorado to become acclimated to the altitude; I was ready for the challenge ahead.

My career as a physical education instructor and the demands of raising four kids had kept me active most of my sixty-seven years. When my husband, Don, died in an automobile accident, my old life crumbled. But I kept pushing forward, learning to be independent. Taking up climbing was the first big step in molding a new Kathleen. I had twenty climbs behind me, including two up Mount Kilimanjaro.

I hoisted my pack—which held three water bottles, snacks, a whistle, a Mylar emergency blanket, and other essentials—and glanced at Jody. Though she was younger, we had about the same amount of climbing experience. I grinned at her, bundled in almost as many layers as I was. With my three waterproof jackets, gloves, sweatpants, and baseball cap, I was prepared for the chilly evening temperatures and sudden storms that could lead to hypothermia.

The July afternoon was bright, making every tree, every rock, every wildflower stand out. I drank in the crisp air and thought of Don. In three days it would be the eleventh anniversary of his death, yet it felt like just yesterday that we were walking through the woods by our summer cottage in Wisconsin. I always felt closer to him when I was out in nature.

By one PM Jody and I were at twelve thousand feet, making good time. We kept a steady distance behind a couple of male climbers we had nicknamed "khaki pants" and "blue backpack." Then we hit the boulder field. It was hard to get any kind of hold at all on the huge, smooth rocks, and even harder to distinguish the cairns (marker rocks pointing out the trail). With each arduous step, I realized the descent would be that much more treacherous. I lagged a good two hundred yards behind Jody. I knew I would never get to the top and back down by nightfall. I leaned against a boulder to catch my breath, staring at my dirt-spattered shoes. *Not going to make it this time, Kathleen,* I told myself, breathing hard. I glanced up the mountain at Jody, who had stopped. I waved her on. "You go. I'll be right here," I yelled and gestured. For the first time in the five years we had climbed together, I wouldn't stand next to Jody on the summit, taking in the view.

I settled down onto a tablelike boulder and rested, feeling my heartbeat slow. I drank some water and wiped the sweat off my neck and face. I dozed and then heard a rustle on the trail above me. Turning, I saw "khaki pants"—eyes intent on the ground—navigating the boulders. *Should I call out?* I glanced at my watch. *No need. Jody will be here soon, and we'll go down together,* I thought. At dusk I began scanning the mountain. *Where is she?* I wondered, my shoulders tightening. I got up and stretched and then sat again to wait for Jody.

She must have missed me, I finally told myself as a cloud blanketed the moon. *Well, I'll just walk down in the morning,* I decided. A cold raindrop brushed my ear and soon I was in the midst of an icy shower. I nestled between two large boulders, yanked down my cap, and pulled my blanket close. Then I drew my knees up to my chest, wrapped my arms around them, and fell into a fitful sleep.

The next morning, I looked into the cloudless sky. I was on my own. *Part of the adventure,* I thought, to rally myself. I got up and surveyed my surroundings. I checked my supplies. Then it hit me. Jody had our only map. Now what? I would have to make it down solo, but who better to rely on than myself?

I walked for two hours along the edge of the boulder field, carefully picking my way among the rain-slickened rocks. I had thought I had gotten the hang of it, but then I slipped and my feet shot from under me. I landed hard on my backside and started sliding slowly, painfully down the mountain. I leaned back into my pack to keep from tumbling head over heels, but I kept picking up speed, bouncing over the scree. Abruptly, I hit a tangle of bushes. I grabbed some branches and halted my slide and then crawled to a jutting rock shelf. The seat of my sweatpants was in shreds. I picked myself up and then turned around.

What I saw made me gasp. Above was a forty-five-degree slope the length of two football fields, littered with loose rock. Climbing it would be impossible. The only practical alternative was to stay put.

Strangely, I didn't feel panicked. *Jody will have reached the bottom by now,* I told myself. *Help is on the way. I just have to wait.*

I ate raisins. I watched the sun crawl across the sky. Occasionally I blew my whistle. Around noon, I took the last sip of water from the third bottle. In the distance to my right, a creek shimmered. Far above me, snow glistened like diamonds.

I settled down on a bed of pine brush for my second night on the mountain.

The next morning, I braced myself against a rock and swung my stiff legs back and forth to get the blood flowing. I was parched, but all I had left were my snacks. I unwrapped the peanut butter and jelly sandwich I was supposed to have had for lunch the first day and took a bite. Without saliva, it was like trying to chew wood. I spit it out. I just had to have water. That afternoon it came.

The sky darkened rapidly. Lightning ripped the sky. I cupped the blanket on my lap to form a pool and plunged my face into the water, lapping it up like an animal. I collected pool after pool, directing each into a bottle. As the storm abated, I spied helicopters far overhead. Too far. Feeling giddy, I closed my eyes and drifted off.

"Kathleen."

I jerked my head up. Don? I extended my arms to him. My husband had come for me. With a start, I opened my eyes and shielded my face from tiny hail pellets. "Don, I'm here!" I cried. A dream. But it had seemed so real! I rubbed my eyes and collapsed back onto the rock. I pulled the thin blanket over me, shivering. *You have got to get off this mountain, Kathleen.*

The next morning, I awoke feeling clammy and achingly alone. It was July 28, the eleventh anniversary of Don's death. In my mind I replayed our lives together: the way he had gazed into my eyes at our first dance, the time he repainted a bedroom for Valentine's Day, how he held me after our youngest set out on her own. I smiled at the thought of his dresser drawers, neat enough to pass a military inspection; his strong hands polishing all the shoes in the household and lining them up at the top of the stairs; the silly songs he sang on family road trips. It was like watching a wonderful movie—until the tragic ending. Don could never have seen it coming: A boy adjusting his tape deck missed a stop sign and slammed into his car.

Now I, who had prepared meticulously for this climb, found myself stranded and helpless. Another senseless situation. I still felt amazingly calm and not especially weak, but I knew there was a limit to how long anyone could survive thirst, hunger, and exposure. Would I die on the same day as Don? Or would God help me to find my way as He had after Don's death? "Thy will be done, dear God," I murmured. I settled into my usual position, with my arms wrapped around my knees, and went to sleep.

The next morning the sun shone warmly and dried my clothes. I used safety pins to mend the tears in my pants and exercised the best I could.

I looked up. Helicopters! I grabbed my mirror and tried to catch the sunlight so I could use the reflection as a signal, but it was too small to do much good. I picked up my silvery blanket and waved it frantically. Throughout the day, helicopters swooped nearby, only to rise again out of sight. My hopes sank with the sun. My fifth night on the mountain.

It was quiet the next morning, with no helicopters whirring overhead. *They've given up,* I thought. Still, I struggled to exercise my limbs.

Then I heard a sound. I looked up. A helicopter was right above me. Within seconds I was being lifted by a tall young man. "I've got you; you're okay now," he said.

I let myself go limp in his arms. *It's over.* I was rushed to Vail Valley Medical Center, where I was treated for dehydration and minor abrasions.

Jody was waiting for me. She had followed someone she thought was me—maybe "blue backpack"—out of the boulder field. People, dogs, and helicopter crews had combed the mountain for me, though no one had thought I could survive for six days. "Everyone said it was impossible," Jody told me. I felt proud of myself—I had kept my cool. My training and experience had paid off when it counted. But something nagged at me, as if there were more to it than that.

When I flew home to St. Louis, I was greeted by a cheering throng carrying balloons, banners, and flowers. I rushed into my children's embraces. Relatives and friends told me over and over, "I prayed for you."

Cards and letters from acquaintances and strangers filled my mailbox. "We prayed for you," they said. People who recognized me from the media coverage said, "Hey, are you Kinderfather? I prayed for you."

Is that why I felt so calm? I wondered.

A few days after I got home, my teenaged godson Patrick visited me. "Weren't you scared?" he asked.

"No, I was wrapped in prayer," I said, putting my arms around myself. Suddenly I realized that was the same position I had sat in on the mountain. A feeling of warmth enveloped me, as if I were being embraced at once by everyone who had prayed for me. All along, I'd been protected. It was the last piece of the puzzle.

Today when I go climbing, I still prepare meticulously, but I remember I am never truly on my own. God was there guiding me after I lost Don, and He was there to protect me when I was stranded. I'm proud of my self-sufficiency, but now I pay special attention to the prayers I and my loved ones offer to God—they are the most important supplies I carry.

THE GREAT GRAY YEARS by Ardis Whitman

Once, when I was a little girl in a Nova Scotia parsonage, a charming elderly gentleman came to dinner. Lame from arthritis, he had trouble getting up from his chair at the table. He caught me staring at him with—I am sure—pity and dismay, and he smiled. "Oh, it's not so bad being old," he said. "You'll find that out one day. And I'm going to tell you something you must never forget. There's a hidden treasure out there, and you may not find it until you are at least a little bit old."

At the time, I didn't know what he meant, although I did know what a treasure was. It was something far more wonderful than anything else—something that, in the fairy tales, you looked for endlessly even if you had to go through many perils to find it. Now that I find myself in the territory where the treasure is, I think I know what he meant. At least I know what it is for me. The treasure I have found, the treasure that comes in its full brilliance only when we have learned and lived and loved for many years, is the radiant light of the spirit.

When we are young, the gentle voice of the spirit—that of God in us—is often smothered by our struggle to succeed in a harsh, competitive world. But as we grow older, there is less haste, less need for power; and it is easier to listen and understand. Then, in the last third of our lives, we are able to put together what we know of the universe and the human heart and bring from that learning something to help the world. Our later years are enhanced by lessons learned over the span of a lifetime, lessons taught by pain, grief, and joy. I think, for example, of the most serious illness of my life, the hard days filled with painful tests, the light coming in from hospital windows that looked out on a flowering park and picnicking families, my fear that I would never be part of that world again.

I remember the anguish after the death of my husband and, so soon thereafter, the loss of a beautiful son—a minister who responded to us and to his parishioners with a never-failing love.

And I remember family times when we were still all together, laughing and at ease; moonlight on the Acropolis in Athens; the piercing beauty of a lonely beach at twilight in Nova Scotia; the times when God seemed as closely present as my own hand. These accumulated human experiences, which all of us have, give us resources of strength and wisdom. We discover that the mind and spirit can overcome physical illness and heal emotional pain. We learn about failing and trying again, about love and how we earn it, about God and how we reach Him in prayer and discover His will for us.

The years are like a diamond cutter, striking away the shapelessness, leaving behind the essence of the self. They teach us to be responsible and adequate and reasonably brave.

In the last third of life, we see what we couldn't grasp when we were young because we hadn't learned enough. In fact, older people are particularly adept at synthesis. Studies show that the younger brain can handle "bits" of information faster than the older one; but the mature brain "more readily processes 'chunks'— that is, it forms concepts based on the greater store of bits."

As a result, we can better understand life's unities. We see how past, present, and future melt into each other, lead to each other, since now we can look back on life as a whole. We have had time to see that our lives are tied to the network of life everywhere; that what each of us does affects others, and they, in turn, affect the people in their lives; that life and death spring from each other and are one as the dying of leaf and flower in the fall is followed by the resurrection of springtime.

The trouble is that no one taught us to expect this last and greatest fulfillment. No one said when we were growing up that the journey of life could be a constant widening of horizons, a continuous rebirth, a steady moving toward the supreme prize, the life of the spirit.

So it often happens that we do not recognize the treasure when we come upon it, nor know how to use it. And then we miss what these years have to teach us. That is too bad, because the long segment of life after the productive years must be part of God's plan. Like all the rest of life, it must have been given to us for a purpose.

What must we do to fulfill that purpose—to use to the utmost this time of the spirit, this crowning glory of our lives?

We must set aside time for spiritual growing. When I feel confused and tired, when my heart runs dry, I go, if I can, to sit by the sea or in an empty church or cathedral—a solitary place where I feel I can touch the eternal, find easier access to the hidden places in myself.

Some very old civilizations have understood the importance of such withdrawal. In classical Hindu practice, when men and women reach the older years, they are encouraged to unburden themselves of active responsibilities for family and community and to use this time for solitary, spiritual growing.

Most of us cannot leave our families and communities for long periods of time, but we can take short periods daily for meditation and prayer. And when I say prayer, I mean prayer on your knees. For this seemingly small gesture, unimportant in itself, calls attention, summons silence, helps us to concentrate on what we are doing.

Does God answer prayer? Of course He does. Someone once wrote, "Who rises from a prayer a better man, his prayer is answered." Prayers of petition, too, are often answered, as a loving Father answers His children.

Nevertheless, there is much more to prayer than that. Prayer is a dialog, not a monolog. We pray, wrote the thirteenth-century mystic, Meister Eckhart, "so that God may be born in our souls." And those who have the patience and courage to listen as well as to ask—and the willingness to hear God's answer—will find their spiritual life growing steadily day by day.

We also grow spiritually by seeking fellowship—people who are traveling the same road. And what a wonderful time it is to look for them! In the last decade or two, millions of people, like hungry children looking for bread, have joined the search for the spirit. They are flocking to Bible study, to retreats and meditation centers, to caring churches.

If you look, you will find groups and organizations, too, that have come together for this purpose. One of the very best I have found is the Phoenix Club, a national organization that calls itself the Last Third of Life Club. Its members hold weekly discussion meetings to share experiences in the growing of the spirit: to "talk large talk rather than small talk; to talk about things that matter rather than things that don't." Seek the spirit, too, by turning to the recorded wisdom of past and present. Open your Bible—that change-making, transforming book. Everything is here of human struggle, loss and despair and hope; of the coming of love to the world and of the kingdom of heaven. Jesus said, "The kingdom of heaven is like treasure hidden in a field, which a man found and covered up; then in his joy he goes and sells all that he has and buys that field" (Matthew 13:44, RSV).

Great art, too, and great books and music often speak God's message. Go to the museum and find a picture of the intricate structure of a flower—or a deserted and lonely house or the face of a noble man or woman—and study it until you feel you understand something you didn't understand before.

Look afresh at the lovely world around you. The world is God's and His beauty and love speak in all living things, waiting to be recognized and experienced. "Above the whole of God's creation," said a speaker at the World Council of Churches in Vancouver in 1983, "we may write the words 'God so loved.'" The mystic Evelyn Underhill said it in singing lines:

> I come in little things,
> Saith the Lord:
> Yea! on the glancing wings
> Of eager birds, the softly pattering feet
> Of furred and gentle beasts...

One day not long ago I sat at my desk in front of an upstairs window, a window that looks out on the passing life of the street as well as on great trees and flying birds. It was spring—that blessed season when the wild things seem to feel closer to human homes and hearts.

At any rate, one small bird did. It flew straight to my window and, clinging to the narrow sill outside, peered in, its bright eyes less than two feet from mine. For a full minute, we sat, both of us motionless, seemingly trying to fathom each other's identity. And then he flew away and left me feeling deeply touched by this unexpected bond between us, by the oneness of all living things.

Greet day and night with joy, taking from each moment its quota of beauty and tenderness. Go to the window at midnight and see the moonlight lighting the clouds and falling on the quiet street; get up early and watch the dawn spread like feathers of fire across the sky.

"Use your eyes," said Helen Keller, "as if tomorrow you will be stricken blind." For if you look long enough at anything—the multiform tracery of winter trees; the behavior of a flock of birds in spring and fall; the formation of a flower or a snowflake; clouds on a summer day—you will have found a piece of the treasure, a revelation of the intricacy and beauty God has woven into His world.

And remember that no one else has ever seen it in just the same way! No one else has ever looked through your eyes or heard with your ears or understood in just the way your experience has taught you to understand. You have something original to give just by seeing truly, just by hearing.

Explore the ways of love that you have learned through the years. In my heart, I can still hear the words of my dear son in a farewell sermon in one of his pastorates. "What survives all changes of time and place," he said, "is the magic that occurs when people, in honesty and love, share themselves with each other."

He is right. Only by loving and helping each other can we be truly ready for the spiritual kingdom. Love is important because it brings us close to each other—and that closeness leads us to God, Who is the center and source of all love.

There are those who think that love is harder to come by as you grow older, I remember an old lady who lived next door to us when I was a young mother. She was a very interesting person, but she hid beneath a veneer of bitterness and hostility. "I keep to myself," she said, "because nobody loves you when you are old."

What nonsense! I had just lost my mother and I was living a thousand miles from old friends and family. I would have given anything right then for a surrogate mother—someone who listened and comforted. Now, at this peak of our lives, we are uniquely able to be primarily the giver, the shelter, the listener, the comforter.

A twelve-year-old girl I know said good-bye with tears to a visiting grandmother. "What's good about grandmothers," she said, "is that they always want to hear what's happened to you, and you can talk about it as long as you like." That's as it should be. We should be the perfect listeners—a sounding board for the thoughts of others. Surely we have learned something now—by our mistakes and by our successes—about how to meet the inevitable conflicts in relationships, about how to sustain a love through the divisive years. And the long experience of shared joy, shared sorrow—yes, and shared anger—should qualify us to say, "This is what people are like. . . . this is what is right and wrong about the way we relate to each other. . . . these are the ways of love."

So, now, in the older years, make yourself a place of safety and hope for the people around you. Commit yourself, not just to neighbors and friends, but to a needy world. Where there is pain and injustice, you can help even if you are in a wheelchair—you can write letters to those in power. What matters is that God's love shines through us as the sun through a skylight.

Seek the treasure in your own growing. What a mistake it is to think that as we get older, we should cease to grow! It's a temptation, true. Growing is painful at any age. How easy it is to drift along on the surface; cling to old memories; ask everything around us—from church to neighborhood—not to change!

But this way lies the end of life, for life is change and rebirth. Moreover, by growing we fulfill the will of God. It is apparently God's plan that all things grow until they die. People who relish their later years look to the future, always ready to accept new pieces in the puzzle of life.

Grow! And measure your spiritual growing as you would any other kind. If possible, keep a journal. Through the years, I have done that and I can go back to it now and find in it all the falterings and the failings, all the struggling and the growing, all the people I loved and didn't love and what I learned from them. Look inward, too, as you check your growing, for what is trying to emerge in your life. Are you more understanding than you were a year ago? more loving? more forgiving? more appreciative of the world around you?

Finally, make your peace with death. We need to understand that this, too, is part of God's world, that life and death are one. I once heard someone say, "I never think about the future life. It has nothing to do with my life here and now." Is that really so? Does it really not matter now whether we think of ourselves as perishable dust...or as the housing of an eternal spirit? In a discussion group I was leading years ago, I asked for the definition of a human being and one woman in the group said, quickly and certainly, "A body that the spirit makes human."

Think of yourself not as immortal in some future time, but as immortal now—a sturdy spirit for whom death, when it comes, will be a continuum of the growing of your lifetime.

The last third of life can illuminate all the rest of it—illuminate, crown, and shape it. Through these years, the inner light can grow from one candlepower to the blaze of the sun, warming and blessing everyone around you.

The elderly gentleman I met as a child was right. There is a treasure in the older years, a treasure infinitely valuable. And when we acknowledge it and use it, we not only help ourselves but contribute immensely to the world. For by our individual prayers, our search for the kingdom of heaven, we help to sustain and nourish the growing of the spirit for all mankind.

4 FAITH ... NURTURE YOUR SPIRIT

There is a time for everything,
and a season for every activity....

—ECCLESIASTES 3:1

HOW TO WELCOME OLD AGE by Emilie Miller

Happy Birthday, Mom!" said a young acquaintance to me on my eightieth birthday. "How does it feel to be old?"

"To be old?" I replied. "Young man, this is a question I cannot answer for all aged people; but, speaking for myself alone, it is the fulfillment of a verse from Robert Browning:

'Grow old along with me! The best is yet to be.'"

Now, I haven't felt that way always. A great many years ago, my first gray hairs had set me to thinking quite differently, and I had begun to take stock of myself. What could I do to stay the approach of Father Time? Pluck out the gray hairs? Massage away the tiny wrinkles beginning to show upon my face? Take more exercise? Pay more attention to my expanding figure? Eat less?

All of these things I did try—with commendable vigor. And with the improvement of my appearance came a lift to my morale. However, I avoided old people, for the very thought of "growing old" was a nightmare to me.

Then, one day it happened. Old age was coming to dwell in our home, in the form of my mother-in-law. And she was not only old, but blind too!

Long a widow, she had made her home with her only daughter, who had been stricken with a sudden heart attack and had just passed away.

When Mother Hartsease arrived after the funeral, I had her room ready for her, although I felt keen resentment at her coming occupancy of it. How was I to take care of her, an old woman— and blind! She would have to be "entertained," since she could not see to read or write or do anything else to amuse herself.

Yet, I must tell you that that handicapped old woman proved to be the greatest blessing that ever came into my life, for it was she who taught me how to meet old age with a smile.

Of course, her grief for her daughter was deep and sincere, and the adjustment to new surroundings must have been a severe strain upon her; after the first few days of talking things over, and becoming acquainted with each other, she seldom mentioned her daughter again. Instead—I often would find her in her room, kneeling beside her bed with clasped hands, "talking to God," as she put it. After such a session I had never seen such poise as she then exhibited.

One day I found her in the rocking chair reserved for her on our front porch. Surrounded by a group of small boys and girls, children of the neighborhood, she was telling them stories. I stopped to listen. This story was about Paul, the apostle, his travels, his adventures, his shipwreck. Every day after that, the children came. To hear pirate tales by Robert Louis Stevenson,

Bible stories, fairy stories, historic and patriotic lore, breathtaking adventure stories. How the children loved them! And how she adored her young audience!

Sometimes she would sit at the piano and play a favorite hymn or—humming softly as she played—the old, nostalgic "Love's Old Sweet Song."

I was amazed to find how little entertaining she needed. Indeed, it was she who kept us entertained with reminiscences of her former active life, her recital of poetry, and her general knowledge. As to waiting upon her, I came to enjoy doing for her the little things she could not do for herself.

Finally I unashamedly faced the fact that everything that lives and grows, reaches the peak of its existence in time; after that, its powers inevitably begin to decline. Having reached that peak myself, I began to conserve my health by a more reasonable way of living—less strenuous physically, more active mentally.

With Mother Hartsease as my example, I began to store my mind with worthwhile literature; to read my Bible more assiduously and to put into practice its precepts; and through her I learned to pray, to "talk to God" in reality instead of repeating prayers by rote, like the multiplication table.

I took up a hobby too—raising African violets; I also joined a garden club, where I could meet with other garden enthusiasts and discuss my hobby.

Today, I am able to face the future without fear. When my eyes grow too dim to distinguish the faces of loved ones, and my ears can no longer hear the voices around me, and my tired body longs for rest, I shall welcome with confidence the summons of the Master. Until then, I believe I shall always find this life rewarding, even if I live to be a hundred!

LIVE WELL LONGER by Rosie Schaap

It was early on a chilly Monday morning. A shock of a storm had swept through the Northeast the night before, leaving patches of ice on the pavement and a gray cast in the skies. I carefully navigated the treacherous sidewalks. My knees had been bothering me lately—in my midthirties, I was starting to feel the wear and tear that comes with aging—and another fall would be the last thing I needed. (I had banged up my shoulder the year before by slipping on some steps.) I was heading to New York's Grand Central Terminal to catch a train to New Haven, Connecticut, to interview the writer and veteran surgeon Sherwin Nuland. By e-mail, Shep, as just about everyone calls him, offered to meet me at the station. "When you're off the train, follow the crowd to an escalator, at the top of which you'll see an old man, namely me," he wrote. "I'm average height, average appearance, and average amount of hair atop my head."

It's hard to think of Sherwin Nuland as average. He's written ten books, enjoyed a distinguished career in medicine, and is a clinical professor of surgery at the Yale School of Medicine. He accomplished all this after growing up in poverty in a cramped four-room apartment in the Bronx, occupied by six members of his Jewish immigrant family. I'd wanted to meet him ever since I read his best seller and National Book Award winner, *How We Die: Reflections on Life's Final Chapter.* In unsparing and often graphic prose, Nuland delivers a compassionate and humane account of how our bodies shut down—how we die—told largely through personal stories culled from his decades of practicing medicine. The cumulative effect of these stories, and Nuland's reflections on them, is not to frighten readers but to deepen our understanding and help us confront with open eyes a subject that is often painful to discuss.

On the train, I re-read chapters of Shep's new book, *The Art of Aging: A Doctor's Prescription for Well-Being.* Like *How We Die*, it's told mostly in stories—and tackles a topic most of us tend to joke about more than really talk about.

That "average appearance" business? Shep was just being humble or funny. For a man of seventy-six, he's in great shape, with vibrant blue eyes and, I would say, a better-than-average head of white hair. We talked in the cozy kitchen of the rambling gray clapboard house he shares with his wife, Sarah, a theater director and actress. "Take that one," Shep said, offering me the best seat in the house—a comfy wing chair. He settled into another one beside me, while Sarah set coffee and gingersnaps on the weathered wooden table. I asked Shep why he had decided to write about aging.

"It was about time! You can't be a physician for thirty years without thinking a lot about your body. I'm a student of the human body. We all are, in a sense. The only difference between me and most other people is that I have some technical knowledge. So it's easier for me to understand the science. And like all good med students, I learned early on to observe my own body very carefully."

I laughed, thinking of some doctors I know who seldom exercise and seem to survive on candy bars and coffee. "Doctors do observe their bodies carefully," Shep clarified, "but that doesn't mean they do anything with their observations! When you've been someone who subjugates disease for decades, you can't believe it will subjugate you."

But it's not just observations about his physical health that led Shep to write about aging. He's noticed other shifts. "I've also been observing changes in my relationships with people."

"Like what?" I asked.

"They deepen as we age. I think our relationships become more meaningful. Even new relationships are characterized by caring about others. You're much more empathetic as you get older and come to have a greater understanding of what you mean in the lives of others."

"So there's a lot to look forward to," I said.

He agreed, and we talked about some of the people profiled in *The Art of Aging* who made significant changes in their lives. People like Hurey Coleman, a sixty-four-year-old machinery operator and grandfather of seven who had suffered a massive stroke years before. He hadn't paid attention to his physical health then, but now he diligently applied himself to his demanding course of physical therapy. His motivation? He needed to get back to work to support his family. What gave him strength was his faith in God. "I have great faith in faith," Shep said. "It's my experience that people with great faith accomplish things they wouldn't be able to accomplish without that faith."

Belief in oneself is also essential. Consider Ruby Chatterjee, an Indian woman from Calcutta who contacted Shep after reading *How We Die*. In an eloquent, wrenching letter she explained that her vision and hearing were failing. She could no longer be as independent as she once was. Ruby was considering ending her life. Shep put pen to paper. "You must live for the sake of those who love you," he wrote, "because they need you." A lively friendship in letters was born. Now, Ruby travels widely to spend time with her family, remains an active letter writer, and has even visited Shep on a trip to the States. Her physical challenges have not diminished, but her self-image has changed dramatically—and that's made a huge difference.

Shep's beliefs come not just from professional experience, but from life experience. "In midlife I was profoundly depressed," he said. "I went through electroshock therapy. I was in a mental hospital for thirteen months."

"Did you see a way out?" I asked.

"I always knew I'd get out of it. I kept a photograph of my children in the drawer. And I used to periodically open it up and look at my kids and say to myself, 'It's for them, I've got to do this. This is like Ruby's story: We live for other people.'" When Shep emerged from the hospital, he had no money. His wife at the time had filed for divorce. "I had nothing," he said. "But ever since, I've felt we all have it in us to find the way out of the worst difficulties. When you've been through something like what I went through, you won't take no for an answer from others, because you know they can do it too."

And that is the message of *The Art of Aging*: If we want to live well and age well, we must participate in our own lives. Shep says, "Sometimes it helps to look ahead and ask, 'What do I want to be like five years from now? What do I have to change?' I have to force myself to go to the gym. But once I'm there, I feel better. You've got to start, to grab yourself by the scruff of the neck and do it!"

That goes for staying active mentally, socially, and spiritually too. Shep is a great believer in keeping the mind active through reading—your local paper, the Bible, books you discover when you're browsing at a bookstore or the library. Socially, there's no shortage of groups for people to get involved with—at their churches, temples, community centers. "Many people complain about loneliness, but are reticent. They say, 'I'm not the sort of person who does that.' Then they join a reading group or start to volunteer and are amazed to see that over a cup of tea, there are things to talk about, and they start caring about other people. The lesson is always the same: You've got to do something."

I glanced out the picture window. The morning's gray skies had brightened and the ice was melting in the backyard. "Lo and behold," Shep said. "The sun is shining. It's clear and light. It's a great day." I agreed. Shep made me think, a lot. I can decide to go to the gym more. I can set aside time for reading. I can decide to love the people in my life more, to be there for the people who love me.

Back on the train, I thought more about my conversation with Sherwin Nuland. *Yes, the body weakens as we age, yet the spirit grows stronger. Our faith strengthens and our beliefs—in self, in family*

and community, in the goodness and worth of others—deepens. And
in that deepening, we grow old well.

SEASONS OF LIFE by Elizabeth Sherrill

I didn't think, as we stepped into the bleak little restaurant, that I
would leave it carrying a gift from God.

It was February, a midweek night, and the forlorn café on
the dusty outskirts of Brignoles, in southern France, was the
only eating place open. It was just the sort of spot—my husband, John, and I reminded ourselves—where we had eaten all
the time in our early days over here. *We were young,* I thought.
More adaptable.

Our host, who was also the chef and the sole other diner,
brought us a platter of gristly looking meat, and with a cordial
"Bon appétit!" went back to his own meal.

"Remember how hungry we'd be after biking all day?" I said
to John as he sawed valiantly at the meat. In our younger days we
hadn't needed a car to travel around in. We had a lot more energy
then.

Something else was different too—years ago we would have
struck up a conversation with the friendly proprietor, maybe discovered a fascinating story. He was a small, stooped, bright-faced
individual, dressed in the jacket of a blue suit and the pants of a
brown one. It would be hard to talk about anything very complicated now; we had forgotten a lot of our French. Your memory
starts to go as you get older.

Thinking back came naturally just then. This was 1997, an anniversary trip exactly fifty years after John and I had met and married here. But if memories were welcome, comparisons were not. The contrast was too great between that young bride and the gray-haired woman who had looked back at me from the cracked glass in the restaurant washroom.

All day we had driven through a lifeless winter landscape, the freshness of spring long past. I remembered silently asking God as we traveled along roads lined with leafless poplars, *What is this season of life for? Just…looking back?*

"Café?" the little proprietor asked as he picked up our plates.

Soon we heard the hiss of steam, which meant a strong black espresso was brewing. Several minutes passed but no coffee appeared. At last the man emerged from his pocket-handkerchief of a kitchen, two small coffee cups in one hand and in the other a great sheaf of feathery leaves dotted with round yellow flowers.

"Pour vous, madame!" he said, presenting the spray to me with a Gallic flourish.

I took the astounding branch from his hand—lacy fernlike leaves and a hundred bright pom-poms lit the shabby room like so many miniature sunbursts.

"Why…where did these come from!" I marveled.

"From the garden." He gestured toward the back of the building.

Now? In February?

"A greenhouse," John guessed.

"Mais non!" From his garden, our host insisted. He waved his hand again. "Out there."

"But," I protested, "nothing's blooming at this time of year!"

"Why yes, madam! Acacia blooms all through the year. Always it has flowers. Summer, winter—every season."

Acacia blooms in every season. . . .

The proprietor drew a chair up to our table; suddenly we found ourselves talking like old friends. And in the morning in our hotel room basin, the acacia flowers had opened wider, so wide it seemed impossible that a single branch could hold so many blossoms. A brand-new day stretched ahead, with a hundred new things I wanted to explore and do.

Not the same things I had done fifty years ago. My memory wasn't as sharp perhaps, my energy less. But today was today—with different insights, different adventures. A time for the flowering of the season at hand.

WHY GIVE UP JUST BECAUSE YOU SLOW DOWN?
by Adela Rogers St. Johns

I've lived in a dizzy whirl of drama from the day I went to work on a newspaper three quarters of a century ago. Hurry up! Hurry up! Hurry up! has been the beat I've marched to since I chased my first fire engine at age sixteen. Years later, even after I'd become a grandmother, my city editor still called me "Swifty."

"Swifty," he'd bellow across the city room, "the Lindbergh baby has been kidnapped. Go out and scoop the town."

Or William Randolph Hearst, owner and publisher of all those papers, would be on the phone at midnight. "King Edward has entertained Mrs. Simpson at Buckingham Palace. This is serious. Leave for London in the morning."

When I became a great-grandmother, I was still "Swifty," still felt I could "scoop the town," and often did. I still think I can. Nothing or no one can make me feel old.

But at ninety, God sends me a distinct message. It, too, comes in loud and clear. "Slow down! Slow down! Learn the unlearned lessons—patience, for starters. Change from a wild jitterbug tempo to a stately minuet." Harder still, for one who has thrived on excitement: "Learn to sit still."

It hasn't been easy. The lessons we need to learn seldom are. But now my body insists on it.

Once upon a time, I lived in a lovely home we called The Hill, and was the proud possessor of a newfangled and temperamental garage door. At a gentle touch, the door was supposed to lift onto rails and tuck itself away under the roof. Only sometimes it didn't. It derailed. A friend of mine, a former all-American and pro football coach who prided himself on his physical prowess, used to show off his strength by lifting that thing back on track. Came the day when he bent to raise the door—and couldn't.

Cal was stunned. Humiliated. Defeated.

"Well," I said airily, "sooner or later we all find we can't move the piano alone. And there's no reason why we should. Just accept it, my friend."

I was to remind myself of those words when the time came that I couldn't hoist a box of books, or a forty-pound, squirming great-grandchild, or even carry my own typewriter. But I hadn't recommended resignation to Cal, which is a negative, quitting quality—meaning to abdicate, surrender. I'd come out for positive acceptance—to take, to receive willingly.

Today, I've accepted. I find I can still do all the important things I ever did, but slowly. Differently. Sometimes the doing requires ingenuity, which adds the lesson of perseverance to patience.

Take this piece I am writing for you now. "Swifty" would have sat down at the typewriter and dashed it off in no time. My back and my typewriter chair are no longer compatible. So "Grammy" sits in an armchair with an improvised lapboard, pencil, and legal pads, and writes in longhand.

The book I'm working on, one I've dreamed of doing all my life, is taking months longer than I'd figured. My editor calls and asks tactfully, "Anything I can do for you?"

And I reply, "Cultivate patience along with me," which, bless him, he does.

Long ago I became the first woman reporter ever admitted to the all-male press box at a major sports event. If I wasn't in the press box, I was at ringside for a championship fight, or the infield tower for the Indianapolis 500.

Well, I haven't lost my zest for sports. And I still have a ringside seat: via TV. I can sit in my chair, and if all my friends and relations are busy, I'm perfectly content to be an audience of one. You should hear me cheering, rooting, carrying on as if I were there in the crowd.

When I lived in New York, I rarely took a taxi because I liked to walk. I still do. My walking stick reminds me that I'm not to run or jog or even walk without pausing now and then. But it's a good companion. I frequently stop to lean on it while I take a really good look at a flower, a tree, a little boy building a mud dam.

I was doing exactly that the other day when the little boy threw mud at me and yelled something rude. My newly imposed patience kept me from taking my stick to him just long enough for me to remember that the insult wasn't personal. There have always been rude little boys. In fact, he made a nice contrast to the polite youngster I met at the next corner who offered to help me cross the street. I thought of the old story about the Good Deed wherein the Boy Scout helped the old lady to cross the street when she didn't want to go. I hadn't meant to cross that street either, but if this boy wanted to help me, then I decided I wanted to let him.

For that's another thing I've had to accept. Help. As my friend the football player finally had to accept help with the garage door, so I've had to accept help crossing the street, getting into and out of cars, bathing, dressing. Mr. Hearst once decided to make me the best-dressed female reporter in the country. He paid for it, but I did all the rest. Today if I turn up the well-dressed ancient, you may be sure my granddaughter Kristen, who lives nearby, has had a lot to do with it. Still, as an independent, self-reliant career gal, I had to find a solvent that would permit me to accept help like this without embarrassment or loss of dignity.

So I've cultivated gratitude.

I've been fortunate in being lovingly welcomed into the homes of family members. Strangely, that too presents problems. The ego shrieks. At least mine did. Once châtelaine of The Hill, casting bread (and cake) upon the waters, I didn't quite know how to act when it was given back to me. So I've had to learn to receive in the same spirit in which I gave.

And I've learned about memory. I did a television interview here in our living room last week about a long-gone movie star. I had a wonderful time reliving those Hollywood days. I treasure my memories, but not to the point of wallowing—and sinking—into the past. The cure for the homesickness called nostalgia is enthusiasm for today, curiosity about tomorrow. I read the papers, hear the news, keep up with new books, new personalities, try to figure out who's going to be the next Most Valuable Player, or president.

My only real regret is not for the past but for today. I'd give anything to be physically nimble enough to serve as family baby-sitter or to help in a number of other ways. So, there are lots of things I can't do. But this I know. I do not have to give up because my body has slowed down. I can pray, I can love. And with patience, acceptance, perseverance, gratitude, curiosity, I can keep myself alert, active, intact.

I have always cherished words attributed to John Quincy Adams, sixth president of the United States, when he was an old man and a friend greeted him with the customary, "How are you?" The aging statesman took the time to answer truthfully. He was, he said, very well: The exterior body in which he was housed was weather-beaten, winter had left frost on the roof, beams sagged, the joints creaked, and the foundation was no longer quite steady, but "I, John Quincy Adams, am quite all right, I thank you."

So with me.

At fifty I was rash enough to select a verse of Robert Browning as my favorite inspirational quotation:

Grow old along with me!

The best is yet to be,

The last of life, for which the first was made.

Of course, I didn't know then what I was talking about. But today, at ninety, I would choose it again. With understanding. And what is this best?

It is not the nights of serene sleeping I enjoy, knowing no telephone will ring me into frantic action. It is not those stately virtues I've been cultivating to make the years rich. It's not even the great love I share with my family, good as this is.

The best, to me, is something unique to the Great Gray Years, something my grandmother used to call "time to make one's soul." It is that time to sit still. To read my Bible—slowly. To pray and meditate—slowly. To learn the deep meaning of "this is life eternal, that they might know thee the only true God, and Jesus Christ, whom thou hast sent" (John 17:3, KJV).

To use the twilight years to prepare for the great transition, so that when it comes, I can speak from the heart the final words of John Quincy Adams: "This is the last of earth! I am content."

TIME ON THE RIVER by John Sherrill

As we boarded the ship in Antwerp for the journey up the Rhine, I knew I was running away—running away from the fact that moving to a retirement community meant being cooped up with a bunch of old fogies sitting around counting their pills. Of course, I wasn't "one of them," even though what was left of my hair was white and the steps leading up to our stateroom were extraordinarily steep.

Imagine my dismay, on walking into the dining room that first evening, to discover that most of our fellow passengers on the Viking Sun were white-haired too. Sure enough, three people at our table immediately got out their pillboxes.

A very old man with two canes was making his painful way straight toward us. As he lowered himself into the seat next to mine, I read his name tag: Hamilton. A waiter offered to get Hamilton's dinner from the buffet. "Thoughtful of you!" boomed Hamilton with a glorious smile.

I saw that smile often in the next ten days. Hamilton never missed a meal or a shore excursion. He beamed on lace makers and glassblowers and clock carvers. He hobbled down church naves and up castle steps.

Watching Hamilton, I knew that in our new community we'd find other men and women whose physical limitations hadn't squelched their zest for living, inspiration for this next stage of the journey.

TURNING INWARD by Marilyn Morgan King

It's getting harder for me to read. I may soon have to go to large print. My hearing is slowly fading too. My body seems to be gradually closing some of its windows to the outside world as I grow older.

But there's another side to this page of life. As my sensory input diminishes, I'm less easily distracted by external things and more inclined to turn to God's presence within me for nourishment and spiritual companionship. I now have more time to savor silence, to spend an hour sitting on the mountain or by the stream, soaking up God's presence in nature, and to open myself to the life of the spirit in prayer and meditation. Could it be that the dimming of our senses with age is made for this quiet turning inward? I have to admit that it's not an easy time in life. Body parts are wearing out; endurance is diminishing; short-term memory has started to fail. Yet in their place has come the priceless gift of contemplation.

My husband, Robert, and I have decided that now is the best time of our lives! *God of grace and mercy, may I stop dreading the losses of age and accept with thanksgiving the special gifts You have provided for this time in life.*

5 TRUST . . . GOD IS WITH YOU ALWAYS

Trust in the Lord with all your heart,
and do not lean on your own understanding.
In all your ways acknowledge him,
and he will make straight your paths.

—Proverbs 3:5–6 (ESV)

KEEP GROWING by Fred Bauer

Though gray be your hair
With little to part
This does not denote
The age of your heart.
—Michael Franklin Ellis

I may be sixty-five," I heard a man facing retirement say, "but I refuse to be welked." As a writer, I am fascinated by quaint expressions, so I went to my small dictionary to look up the word *welk*. No luck. Further investigation in Merriam-Webster's huge dictionary led me to this definition: "to fade away or dry up." The word, which has German roots, is now obsolete. Paraphrasing Douglas MacArthur's famous quote would make it read: "Old soldiers never die, they just welk."

Everyone over thirty-five has paid some mind to aging, to fading, to drying up. Is there any secret for avoiding it or slowing down the process? "It's simply a case of mind over matter," goes one old saw. "It doesn't matter if you don't mind."

My thought on the subject of welking, for what it's worth, is that humans have three ages—physical, chronological, and mental—and the third is the most important yardstick of all. If you are tuned in to life—still interested, still learning, still enthused about sunrises and sunsets, new births and rebirths, still willing to involve yourself in the lives of others—then you don't need to worry about drying up. You're still vital and growing.

WE'RE TOUGHER THAN YOU THINK by Mary Martin

Four of us were in a taxi headed for a restaurant in San Francisco's Chinatown when the crash occurred. It's the last thing I remember about that September day nineteen months ago.

When I came to in a hospital bed, my daughter, Heller, and my son, Larry, were looking down at me anxiously. I was trying to ask them, "What happened? Where are my friends?" But I couldn't. The pain was too great.

Only later did I learn that a van had smashed broadside into our cab and that my friend and close business associate, Ben Washer, had been killed instantly. Janet Gaynor, my dearest friend, caught the impact of both my body and Ben's and was smashed up inside and fighting for her life. Her husband, Paul Gregory, had a serious whiplash, broken ribs, and a bruised kidney. The driver of the van had been charged with running a red light, drunken driving, and manslaughter.

My pelvis was broken in three places, and I had a punctured lung, fractured ribs, and pain—from head to toe. At the age of sixty-eight, I wondered if life had not dealt me a bitter final blow. Would I ever be able to walk again? Was my career over—again?

How ironic it seemed. Up until the moment of the accident, my life had begun to brighten once more. For a long time after the death of my husband, Richard Halliday, I had been in a dark night of grief. We had been married for thirty-four years. In my despair, I stopped acting and singing; my singing voice had given out completely. But slowly, through the help of my family, and friends like Janet Gaynor—yes, Janet especially—I had found my way out of that darkness.

My new home, too, had played a part in my recovery from grieving Richard's death. On a visit to San Francisco, I fell in love with that city all over again and made up my mind that I wanted to live there. "That's not very practical," Ben Washer had said. "You already have two homes." But I said a little prayer anyway, that if it was all right with the Lord, I'd really like to be in San Francisco. A few days later I was asked to join Jim Hartz as cohost of a TV program. And from what city was that show being telecast? San Francisco.

"Thank You, Lord," I said, "but I really didn't mean to press You all that quickly."

Now, a year later, lying in a hospital bed, I was thinking about that show. Called *Over Easy*, it was designed to interest and help older people—people over forty. We were supposed to tell our audience how to get more out of living in their later years. Talk about irony! Here I was, approaching seventy, in pain, and wondering if life held anything more for me. So what help could I bring to a television audience now? It all seemed so bleak.

Or was it? The more I thought about it, the less bleak it became. I did have something to say. And I learned what it was in that hospital bed.

My cue came from Janet, who was somewhere in the same hospital. Over and over I asked people how she was doing. "She's fighting for her life," they'd tell me. Another time I'd hear, "That little gal has great courage. If she keeps on fighting that way, she'll make it."

Fighting, that's what Janet was doing, fighting hard to live. And why? Because every spark of life that God has breathed into us is precious. Janet knew that; so did I.

Now I wanted to do some fighting of my own, and the first thing I had to do was to take on my most immediate adversary: pain. In the next days, the pain didn't go away, but I came to terms with it. I even turned it into a kind of blessing. When you feel pain, you know that you're alive; and where there's life, there's hope; and where there's hope, you can start doing something with your life!

"I've got to get out of this bed," was the next thing I told myself. "I've got to get out of this bed and go see Janet."

I started by raising myself to a sitting position in bed. It took a while before I could get to the point that they would let me put my feet on the floor. And even then, I was unable to straighten up. I was given a walker and taught how to push it ahead of me, and then shuffle my feet after it. It took a week to learn how to push my way six inches at a time, but little by little—push, shuffle; push, shuffle—I began to get somewhere. And then one day I shuffled all the way to Janet's room!

The moment Janet saw me, her face broke into a big, broad smile. She had eleven broken ribs, a broken collarbone, a ruptured bladder, a bleeding kidney. And she was smiling. I shook my head in sheer wonder.

"No matter how battered," Janet said, still smiling, "it's amazing what the human body is capable of."

"You can say that again!" I said, breaking into a big, broad smile of my own.

Every chance I got, I hobbled my way to Janet's room. When I managed to push the walker twelve inches at a time, I asked the doctor, "How long will I have to use this thing?"

"Twelve weeks or so," he said.

"Twelve weeks!" I shot back. "No way!"

After several weeks in the hospital, I was allowed to go home. I "walked" the fifteen feet from the exit to a waiting car with the walker, but this time I was straightened up. Just as I reached the car door, I heard a lot of noise behind me. I turned to see doctors, nurses, and aides leaning out the windows, cheering, and applauding—and crowing, "We believe."

It made me glow.

My home is one of those wonderful San Francisco houses on one of those wonderful San Francisco hills. When I arrived there with my nurse, Bee Kilgore, I had to figure out how to climb four flights of stairs to my bedroom. I did it by sitting down on the first step with the walker in front of me, and pushing myself up backward, one step at a time, resting at each landing, and then resuming the backward trek upward.

The next day I was eager to get outside. But how to get down those four flights of stairs? "Don't!" Bee Kilgore ordered. "You're sure to fall down."

"Well, how did I get up here? Sliding up backward one stair step at a time. I can slide down forward one step at a time." And so I did.

About a week after I left the hospital, I went back to work on *Over Easy*. I was wearing a brace and pushing my walker as the cameras followed me onto the set and to my seat. After the show, Jules Power, the producer, hurried over to me. "Mary," he said, "you don't have to be on camera while you're going through all that struggle with the walker. We can start the cameras going after you get to your seat."

"Oh no," I said quickly. "What's this show all about anyway? I want people to see how we old folks can get where we're going no matter what we have to do to get there." And I might have added that a lot of people who are disabled could live fuller lives if they'd forget their foolish pride about how they look and make use of the walkers and wheelchairs and hearing aids and other things that can make their lives easier.

In time, with Bee at my side, I took my first walk without the walker. And it was six, not twelve, weeks after the accident!

One day, I even walked a whole block. Only then did it hit me. *Hey, you'll have to walk back,* I said to myself. *That means another block.* But I made it. And one day, I was able to tell Bee, "Please, don't come with me." I walked alone. Five blocks. Pretty soon I was walking a mile.

It still hurts when I overdo. So I wear a sacroiliac belt. But the difficulties don't stop me. Every morning, I'm up at five thirty, and after prayers, I take a walk or swim and then go to work. I'll never stop working. When I can—and I try to be with them often—I'm enjoying my children, my grandchildren, and my friends.

In May last year, I made a special trip to New York to see a special friend, Ethel Merman, who had been operated on for a brain tumor. I never thought I'd ever see her flat out on her back. To me, Merman—then in her midseventies—was like the Statue of Liberty. Indestructible. But there she was in a hospital bed, unable to walk or talk. I wasn't even sure she could hear me. I sat there holding her hand, trying to tell her with my eyes that I was praying for her, willing her strength.

"Look at me, Merman," I finally said out loud. "Promise me you will get up out of this bed and walk and talk again."

The garbled sounds that came from her were saying, I will. I promise. I will.

When I got hack to San Francisco, there was a letter from her son Bob. "Mother is home!" The words rang happily from the page. "Home!" Shortly after that I picked up the ringing phone, and there on the other end of the line was Merman. She'd always been a fighter!

I doubt that there is anybody, really, who doesn't know that all life is a fight, and that sometimes life itself is what we have to fight for. I've never forgotten something that one of our San Francisco columnists, Charles McCabe, once wrote, "The only real sin in the world is not to fight, not to realize the fullness of your own nature."

I think that's what the Lord means when He tells us in Deuteronomy 30:19, "I have set before you life and death, blessings and curses. Now choose life."

I know that nothing is ever going to be quite the same with my body. I was in a terrible accident. I'm getting older. The only thing to do is accept that, move on, and try to help other people. Indeed, whenever I see older people who say, "It's all over. I'm finished," I want to shout at them, "Don't ever settle for that. Your body is tougher than you think—and your spirit is invincible. Choose life! Fight back!"

COME FLY WITH ME by Mary Ann O'Roark

Growing up in a small town in West Virginia, I'd always dreamed of the adventures I would have when I went out into the world. It was 1963, the spring of my senior year at the University of Pittsburgh, when I saw a movie called *Come Fly with Me*, about three young stewardesses and their adventures. One stewardess was always in a predicament of some sort; another was shy, demure and reserved. But it was the third who captured my imagination. She was so elegant, with a serene face and a voice like warm honey. Who was this woman? I wanted to be like her—young and vibrant, in what felt like the most exciting time in history to be young and vibrant.

I read a review of the movie and learned that the actress who had made such an impression on me was Dolores Hart. One critic deemed her the next Grace Kelly. Close to my age, she had already gotten a Tony nomination for a performance on Broadway, and had appeared in a range of movies from *Where the Boys Are* to a costarring role with Elvis Presley in *King Creole*. Dolores Hart—forever linked in my mind to her stewardess character—was everything I wanted to be: attractive, confident, adventurous.

The next week, on my way to class, I noticed a poster in a travel agency's window: "Be a Stewardess, Wing Your Way to Adventure." Ever since I'd been a little girl, I'd prayed to discover the right path for my life. As I saw it, that included travel and adventure, with a marriage and family somewhere along the way. *Come Fly with Me* had made me think a stint as a stewardess was the ideal launching point. I went through a series of interviews with TWA and was hired. After college, I went off to "hostess training," a whirlwind combination of flight academy and charm school. Then, from my base in San Francisco, I flew all around the country. I tied my scarf the same way Dolores Hart had in the movie, and tried to be as gracious and self-possessed as she was. It was hard to imagine that just a few years before, I'd been living with my parents in a West Virginia steel town.

One day, while waiting for passengers to board, a startling headline on a newspaper caught my eye: Actress Leaves Career to Join Convent. Dolores Hart was abandoning her Hollywood life to become a cloistered nun. *Is this a publicity stunt?* I scanned the article, but there weren't any specifics about where she was going, just a quote to the effect that she felt this was where God was leading her. I couldn't help thinking, *Why would an attractive young woman give up a glamorous life to join a convent?*

In the meantime, I was ready for a change of my own. While I loved flying—the roaring shudder as the jet lifted off the runway, the sweep of clouds struck golden by slanting rays of sun, the glitter of stars as I stared out the galley window at night—I hadn't counted on being so jet-lagged and footsore. After a year, I turned in my airline wings.

When I was about ten, I'd put out a neighborhood newspaper from our backyard in West Virginia. In college, I'd majored in writing. I was ready to widen my horizons in journalism. I moved to Manhattan and got a job at *The Saturday Evening Post*.

Eventually I moved on to *Seventeen* and *McCall's*. My love for my work and for the rhythm and color of city life cradled me as surely as the embrace of a small town. Yes, I was living out my dreams, having a grand adventure. Even in my forties, when I came to work at *Guideposts* magazine, I still felt brave and frisky and...young. Then gradually I noticed it happening. When I walked too far in high heels, my knees hurt. I'd glimpse my reflection in a store window and wonder why that older woman was wearing my clothes.

So much of my identity involved being a young woman. I never anticipated that I'd wake up in the middle of my life and be blindsided by the fact that even members of the sixties' "Youth Generation" don't remain young forever. As I approached fifty, I felt disoriented and afraid, even angry. It seemed I'd hit some bumps on "the right path," and the husband and children that I'd expected to share my life with never materialized. Nothing had prepared me for aging—not college, not hostess training, not even my years in the working world. Was there really such a thing as growing older gracefully?

During that time, I walked into a crowded ballroom at a writers' convention and, out of perhaps a thousand people, sat down next to a dark-haired woman who introduced herself as Antoinette Bosco. As we chatted, I felt an unexpected urge to open up to her. "I've been having trouble coping with getting older," I blurted out. "Sometimes I feel so alone and unsure about the future."

"There's a special place I go when I'm feeling like that," Toni said, "not far from where I live in Connecticut. It's called the Abbey of Regina Laudis. I always have a better perspective on things after I've been there. Come visit and I'll take you." In my mind, I pictured a medieval stone edifice on a fog-shrouded mountaintop.

One August afternoon a few weeks later, Toni met me at the bus in Danbury. We drove through rolling hills and woodlands until we reached an opening in the trees and swung into the abbey's small parking area. Instead of the intimidating setting I'd imagined, I saw what seemed to be an old farmhouse with a rustic wooden cross on its roof and a greenhouse as its entryway. A tractor rumbled past, driven by a ruddy-cheeked nun in long skirt and flowing wimple who waved at us merrily. "The nuns run these three hundred and fifty acres as a farm," Toni explained as we strolled along.

"Close to forty sisters live here," Toni went on. "Some came to the abbey after successful careers as lawyers and teachers; one was in the state legislature. They wear full habits and never leave the grounds except for emergencies or special studies." She pointed toward outlying buildings. "Over there are a blacksmith shop and kilns to fire the nuns' pottery. Sister Debbora is a beekeeper; others bake bread, milk the cows, tend the oxen." She told me the sisters had just built a chapel where they gathered to pray and sing eight times a day.

From the far side of a field, a nun appeared and swept down a grassy slope toward us. A wide straw hat with a floppy brim sat on her head over her wimple, sneakers peeked out beneath her long black skirt. Something about her seemed familiar. When she came closer, I caught my breath.

I knew that face framed in an oval of white, but now there was a gentle webbing of lines around her blue eyes and smiling mouth. "Mother Dolores!" Toni said. "This is my friend Mary Ann."

"Welcome," Mother Dolores said in that rich, honeyed voice I remembered so well. "How wonderful to have you here." I sputtered something about being glad to meet her. A gust of wind caught the brim of her hat, and she laughed and held it in place. Like me, she wasn't a girl anymore. But her expression was luminous, her manner exuded contentment and peace. As the bells rang, calling her to afternoon prayer, she invited me to come back to the abbey again.

Some months passed before I was able to return. When I did, I had a long talk with Mother Dolores through a wooden grill that surprisingly only added to the intimacy of our conversation. I poured out how I'd seen her in the stewardess movie, and at the time felt it was a kind of nudge from the Holy Spirit to set me on my path to adventure.

Mother Dolores laughed. She said that it had been in New York, while publicizing *Come Fly with Me*, that she had made her final decision to become a postulant and join the nuns at the abbey. She'd started visiting the abbey several years before, while performing on Broadway. "Subconsciously, something kept drawing me back." she said.

I told her how I'd wished to be as glamorous as she was—and how disoriented I'd felt when I was forced to face the reality of getting older. "Back when I was making movies," Mother Dolores said, "I looked in the mirror one day and realized that if my sense of worth and fulfillment was based on my looks and youth, it was all short-lived." She leaned closer. "I sensed inside there was something more—much more. And I was right. Time and age don't matter."

As I gazed through the grill into her gentle face, it became clear: True beauty comes not from youth or genes or circumstance, but from a wellspring of inner grace that transcends age and environment. "Don't worry," Mother Dolores said. "Wherever you are on your path of life, however unexpected the twists and turns, God continues to draw you to where you belong."

We prayed together and then the bells rang, and it was time for her to go to vespers. As the shadows lengthened, I climbed the hill to the abbey chapel, where the sun's slanting rays bathed the sanctuary with amber light. While the nuns filed in and began to sing, I closed my eyes, filled with a deep feeling of peace. Lifted on the strains of their chanting, I felt older . . . younger . . . ageless . . . safe, an ongoing traveler following God's path as it continues to unfold. Venite . . . jubilate . . . alleluia!

I'd finally discovered what had drawn me to Dolores Hart all those years before. It wasn't glamour or sophistication, as I'd once thought. The Holy Spirit had been leading me to an inner beauty, the eternal beauty of the soul. A beacon that would light my way through the spiritual adventures ahead.

BIRTHDAY BLUES by Sue Monk Kidd

Last August as I drove my twelve-year-old daughter to her first horseback riding lesson, I found myself thinking of the birthday card I'd received that morning from a teasing friend. It pictured three buzzards circling a birthday cake. The caption read, "Forty—the beginning of the end."

It was still a week till my birthday, but already the age jokes had started. I'd tossed the card onto my dresser with a chuckle. But there was just enough truth in it to leave me feeling vaguely troubled. Somehow I'd never thought much about aging, or about how time sweeps so swiftly through its passages. During my thirties, I'd managed to keep alive an illusion that I would be young forever. There would always be time to do everything I wanted. But that wonderful decade—when my children were small and hopes and dreams were young, when everything seemed like a beginning and opportunities stretched forever—was ending.

Maybe it was me, or maybe it was just the fallout of turning forty, but suddenly, bumping along that old country road, I felt an unexpected pang of loss, a sense of ending. It was as if I was standing in the last golden moments of summer just before autumn browned the earth for good.

I let out a huge sigh. It was so big that Ann whirled toward me on the front seat. "What's wrong, Mama?"

"Oh, I don't know. Maybe I should be like Jack Benny and refuse to go beyond thirty-nine," I muttered.

"Who's he?" she wanted to know. I looked at her and felt even older.

As we drove onto the horse farm, I took note of the sign: Omega Farm. *Omega* means "ending." It seemed to be the word of the day.

I gazed through the car window at the red-roofed stables and neatly fenced slopes of countryside. Ann studied them too, moving to the edge of her seat as three young horses came into view. They tossed their chestnut manes in a glaze of sunlight and broke into a gallop. We watched till they were out of sight.

"Mama, where's the plaster horse I painted last year?" Ann asked.

I gave her a curious squint. "It's in that bag of keepsakes in the closet," I answered. She knew the one. It contained all the tender, ragged stuff mothers can never throw away.

"I think I'll hang that horse in my room," she explained.

I smiled. Maybe she was getting into the equestrian spirit after all. Back when I'd first suggested horseback riding lessons, she wasn't enthusiastic. "Try it, Ann. I know you'll love it," I'd coaxed.

"How do you know? Did you ride way back when you were a kid?"

"No, but I always wanted to," I said, remembering. When I was twelve, my room had been filled with shelves of glass horses, books about horses, sketches of horses. Once, in school, I had to write "I will not draw horses in class" one hundred times, but it didn't much cure me. One of my cherished memories is the time my grandmother had taken me to a horse show and I saw those magnificent creatures up close. I watched their exquisite high steps and canters and promised myself I would ride with the same dash and dazzle.

But it had never happened.

Now, with a daughter of twelve myself, that unhatched dream was just another reminder of how old I'd gotten.

At the stable the riding instructor, Barb, was all ready with a sable horse named Whisper. I watched from the shade of a pine tree as Ann climbed into the saddle and floated through the amber dust of that summer afternoon. I noticed the way her eyes widened and her hair bounced back and forth, following her rhythm in the saddle.

As I'd predicted, Ann was delighted with the whole experience. But by the time we arrived home, the delicate melancholy I was feeling had escalated into downright glumness.

That evening, as I sat on the edge of the bed, my eyes fell upon the birthday card that had started the whole thing. It was still on the dresser beside a half-burned candle we'd used a few nights before during a power outage.

I could almost feel time melting away. My shoulders slumped. That's how my husband, Sandy, found me. He sized up the situation immediately. "The birthday buzzards getting to you?" he asked.

"It's embarrassing to respond to a birthday like this!" I answered. "But I feel like something important is ending."

He wrapped an arm around me. "Everybody goes through some reflection when they move into another decade of life. It's natural." Outside, thunder snapped and splinters of light reflected on the windowpanes as if to emphasize his words.

It rained all night. I lay awake, my sudden attack of midlife misery growing darker as the night aged. Oddly, that feeling of misery was laced with images of red-roofed stables and my daughter swaying on the back of Whisper, the horse.

Finally, tired of the whole dreary thing, I began to pray. I told God I was ashamed to be so depressed, but I was really having trouble handling this "beginning of the end" thing. Last of all I mumbled a plea. "Please, God, could You help me?"

The next morning, as I climbed out of bed, for the first time in my life I actually felt old. My back hurt and there were blue shadows under my eyes.

As I trudged into the den I noticed Ann plundering through the bag of keepsakes from the closet. Kindergarten pictures and old letters to Santa were strewn everywhere. She'd found the plaster horse to hang in her room and was now engrossed in the rest of the bag's contents.

"Look, Mama! It's the Me Book I made in third grade."

She handed me an assortment of pages tied together with yellow yarn. On each page was glued a photograph of herself, one for each year of her life.

I thumbed through the short chronology, my eyes wandering over pictures of her as a baby, at one, two, three—all the way up to eight. It was a tiny marching picture of time itself. *Soon—too soon*, I thought, *she will have forty pages also.*

Just then my eyes caught sight of two words at the bottom of the last page. Right where you would expect to see "The End," the teacher had had the students close their books by writing "The Beginning."

I stared at the words as if they had some holy twist, as if they were God's answer to my prayer for help the night before. *This is not the beginning of the end,* He seemed to say, *but the beginning at the end.*

At the window, little pearls of rain still clung to the glass. But inside me things were shifting. Aging, this inevitable collection of pages in my Me Book, could become a journey of diminishing joy unless I remembered that the final words on every page of life were always "The Beginning."

Why, who knows what wondrous new beginning might commence in my forties, I thought. *Or my fifties or sixties or eighties?*

When I took Ann to her next horseback riding lesson, I casually said to Barb, "I don't suppose you have any forty-year-olds taking lessons, do you?"

She saw straight through me. "No, but there's always a first time. Why don't I sign you up?"

My first time atop Whisper, there was such a disparity between my uncorked delight and my antiquated muscles that I literally bounced out of the saddle and onto the ground. Sitting in the dust, I was tempted to wonder if I was kidding myself. I looked up and nothing was circling overhead but God's clean blue sky; the birthday buzzards were gone. I climbed back on the horse and rode till the sun smeared the sky red and dropped behind the trees.

Riding, after all those years, meant a lot more than fulfilling a lost dream. It was my way of living out the truth God taught me. Whether you're ending a year, a decade, a project, or a job—whatever it might be—the truth holds. The end is where you start from.

GETTING MORE OUTGO FROM YOUR INCOME
by Freeman P. Calvert

Nellie and I are living on a fixed income. Living well, I might add. And for a retired man heading into his seventies, that takes some doing—especially these days when you never know what the economy is going to do to you. I can tell you this, however—every day is an adventure for Nellie and me, and we're loving it!

For eight years we've lived in a mobile home park along the Central California coast a few miles south of the town of Arroyo Grande. The park backs up against rolling hills, and we have a sweeping view across a valley to white sand dunes and the sea. Ever since we arrived here, we've found ways to get more "outgo" from our income, and more out of each day for that matter. But coming to this lovely place was not exactly what we originally had in mind.

I retired twelve years ago after thirty years as a law-enforcement officer. Nellie and I were living in Southern California then, and we were determined to get out of the smog and go back to the region of our roots, the Pacific Northwest. I yearned for the hunting, fishing, and clear invigorating air of my youth. Nellie longed for the magnificent scenery of her native Canada. And so we went to live in a mobile home in Sequim, Washington.

It took us a while to find out we'd made a mistake. We had forgotten about the rigorous winters that had been easy enough to shrug off when we were youngsters. Even in Sequim, located in the "banana belt"—a reference to climate, not crops, since only seventeen inches of rain fall there yearly while 150 fall just next door—the blustery winds and bone-chilling cold sent us scurrying back to Southern California from December to March. Besides, Washington was too far away from our two sons and five grandsons, who all lived farther south. And the trips were costly, too, taking money we didn't really have to spare.

Finally, driving our twenty-one-foot, self-contained trailer south into California for the third year in a row, we pulled into a trailer park at Avila Hot Springs. We sat for a while in the winter sunshine, and then Nellie turned to me and said, "Did you ever think that maybe we retired to the wrong place?"

That was something I hated to face. Dreams die hard, especially lifelong ones, unless you have something substantial to take their place. Fortunately, we did. We had the Lord, and our sure trust in His guidance. Every morning, we had our time of prayer and meditation; we thanked Him for each new day and asked that He lead us in the path He wanted us to follow, come what may. When we were off track, things bogged down. When we were on track, life seemed to flow. But we knew we had to listen carefully and do our own footwork.

Hadn't He guided me in Sequim that day of our thirty-sixth wedding anniversary? When I noticed the smoke from my cigarette curling between me and the majestic Olympic Mountains, wasn't His message clear? *You've escaped the smog, and now you yourself are polluting your lungs and My atmosphere.* That day, that moment, I tore my cigarette pack in half and gave it to Nellie.

"Here!" I said. "Here's an anniversary present."

"I've heard that story before," my patient spouse said.

"No," I said. "This is the Lord's doing."

And so it was.

Hadn't He spoken to me through a doctor who said, "If you don't give up alcohol, you'll have an early date in the cemetery"? I'd tried giving that up before, too, but once I realized that it was the Lord's leading, once I had taken the step of actually turning my life and will over to Him, then I knew I could count on His help.

And so it was.

Now, in Avila Hot Springs, bogged down spiritually and materially, we humbly asked Him to lead us in the way we should go.

"How," Nellie wondered out loud as we finished our prayer, "did we happen to wind up here?" It was a good question. Always before we'd driven down Interstate 5 because it was fast and economical.

"Well," I said, "I guess we just decided to take the longer scenic route this time."

"Why did we do that?" Nellie wondered again. "Maybe we'd better do some footwork for the Lord right here."

The steps led us a few miles south to a town we'd never heard of—Arroyo Grande. There, we found this fine new mobile home park under construction. The climate was mild. It was a few hours instead of days away from our children.

So it was that six months later, our old dream abandoned, we moved in and our life began to flow again. We could live comfortably within our income. We owned our mobile home—two bedrooms, two baths, living room, family room/kitchen. We rented the lot, but with it came use of the clubhouse, a pool, and tennis courts, and we had wonderful new neighbors. After visiting around, we found our church home too, the little Bethel Baptist Church. With only 150 members, we could "fellowship" with the entire congregation.

What more could we want this side of Paradise?

Well, the truthful answer was that now we were fixed with a place to live, but what about our fixed income? What about those extras—the little trips, treats, and hobbies we'd looked forward to? If we were to have these, they'd have to come from current savings. And saving on a fixed income embedded in inflation would require ingenuity. That's where the real adventure began. And what fun it has been.

I began to fish for our supper. We enjoy fish on the table and I enjoy the sport. I can go out on the boat at the senior citizen's rate and bring home eight to ten pounds of fillets to freeze. Sometimes it's "bottom fish"—red snapper, lingcod—which is mighty fine eating. When the albacore or salmon run, it's a feast.

Nellie took to clipping coupons, and she did it with more enthusiasm than a blue-chip investor, only hers were the coupons published in the local newspaper and redeemable at supermarkets. After each trip to the grocery, Nellie takes out a calendar and lists what she saves from the careful use of coupons and double coupons. At month's end, she totals her savings, and these are banked in our travel fund.

We discovered that there are exciting bargains in church rummage sales and thrift shops. "Some of our best clothes come from there," Nellie maintains. And they do! New clothes. Merchants who have items left over from sales and don't want to put them back in stock donate them to these worthy causes; it's a treasure hunt to seek and find them. And attending yard and garage sales can be another treasure hunt, a hobby in itself.

For treats, we discovered early-bird dinners whereby good restaurants serve a special menu at a low price between 5:00 PM and

6:00 PM. And a dining club which, for a reasonable initial invest-ment, provides coupons for quality restaurants; pay for one meal, get one free—eat like a king!

We have an exchange system in our park too. There's a box in the clubhouse, available to everyone, where we all deposit store coupons we don't use (all our coupons for cat food, for example, since we're dog people). The exchange works for dining-club members as well. If we have company coming, we swap coupons so each couple has four meals—two free—at one restaurant.

All in all, we've found that there's plenty of exchanging among neighbors in the park, everything from coupons to looking after homes and plants while one couple or another is away traveling. Cooperation is one key to our good life here.

Sometimes I think that the best thing of all about our life on a fixed income is not what we are able to get, but what we are able to give. For one thing, Nellie and I have time to give— I, in counseling, in service projects, and organizations; Nellie as a volunteer at our Community Hospital (over 1,100 hours!). Our neighbors all seem to be givers too. Some Catholic friends walk to seven o'clock mass each morning with a large sack. On the way, they counteract litterbugs by collecting empty alumi-num cans that they redeem for cash to give to the Girl Scouts. One couple collects cash-redeemable newspapers and donates the proceeds to their parish's building fund. An Italian lady buys bell peppers by the crateful at a wholesale house and roasts them to be able to afford the succulent dishes she herself carries to shut-ins.

I know for sure that there are a lot of people a lot poorer than we are who find ways to give. Not long ago a "Hooverville"—a huddle of homeless, "newly poor" families who live in tents, cars, or even just blankets—sprang up on nearby sand dunes. The Christian Women's Club, which meets monthly at various churches, was hard-pressed to stock its food locker to meet the tremendous increase in demand for these people. Then a woman at the Episcopal church came up with an idea. "Each time you go to the market," she said to the congregation, "buy one extra item, no matter how small it is." The response was incredible. The food locker was replenished, and people as poor as the proverbial church mouse felt proud to be able to give something, even a day-old loaf of bread.

That's a lesson I've learned in life: If you think you've nothing to give, you'd better think twice about it!

So that's the way it is, eight years after our moment of decision at Avila Hot Springs. In the twelfth year of our retirement, when Nellie has had her sixty-eighth birthday and I my seventy-first, our sense of adventure has only increased. And why not, since we are willing to follow our Lord one day at a time? Nor do we feel older. How can we, when we firmly believe the motto on our wall: "Remember, this is the first day of the rest of your life."

STEPS IN TIME by Mary R. Mogford

September
First Week: Walk a half mile in fifteen minutes

We felt stealthy, almost like burglars in our own home, as my husband, John, and I padded through our dim, quiet living room. It was all so strange. Normally, at 7:00 AM we'd wake up nice and slow. John would make coffee and bring it into the bedroom on a tray with the newspaper, and the morning news would percolate away on the TV. The lazy life of a semiretired man and his wife.

But instead, this morning we'd pulled on these unfamiliar outfits—sweat suits and jogging shoes—and now we were heading out into the early-day stillness to try our best to walk half a mile in a time limit of fifteen minutes.

Not exactly an Olympic trial? Maybe not for some people. But for me—Mary Mogford, age sixty-four, height five foot three, weight 157—and John Mogford—age seventy, height six feet, weight 235—it was not going to be duck soup. Physically, we were in the pits of condition.

John held the door for me. "All set, shug?"

"I'm right behind you, John L."

Side by side, awkward and self-conscious, we started up Johnson Street. Step. Step. Step. Step. I looked up at John's good face. We'd been married forty-five years, and we were still "that way" about each other. John loves Mary. Mary loves John, John L., Juan, Juanito. I had half a dozen pet names for him. "The light of my life." I wasn't embarrassed to say it. I couldn't picture myself without him.

Step. Step. Step. Step. I matched my pace to John's slower one. Slow or not, we were making a start. Maybe now the awful, nagging, guilty worrying would stop. . . .

For years John and I had dutifully had annual physical check-ups. The doctors never found anything really wrong, though our weight and John's blood pressure kept creeping up.

Then, something drastic had happened. My two sisters died. First, Naoma. Then Nina. Their deaths made me the sole survivor in my family. My parents had died young, my father of diabetes. I'd inherited a susceptibility to the disease from him.

The shock of losing Nina and Naoma caused me to start worrying. My sisters, I felt, had taken poor care of themselves. I began to think about John and me. John's body overlapped his clothes, and he had trouble bending down to tie his shoes. Sometimes he panted for breath and had problems sleeping. He had to keep increasing the amount of his blood pressure medication.

And even though doctors had told me that I had to watch my diet and get regular exercise, I was very slack about it. I didn't like exercising alone, and I could rarely convince John to get into it with me. If he did come for a walk with me, he dragged one foot. Or two. He'd say things like, "I may be walking on the outside, but I'm sitting down on the inside."

As for eating, we really knew how to indulge ourselves. We loved to eat—rich spicy Mexican specialties like thick Texas beef, each morsel coated with "dipping butter." Cooking is my creative art and I'm good at it. My kitchen is like a studio; it has all the latest appliances and gadgets.

Every once in a while I'd talk up diet and exercise. I'd think of all the reasons we had to keep ourselves in tip-top shape. Heading the list were our two children and five grandchildren. But somehow we went on living a sedentary life and eating without restraint and getting fatter. My feeling of apprehension was growing too. I knew we were living dangerously.

October

Fifth Week: Walk one mile in thirty minutes

Step. Step. Step. Step. John and I turned up Johnson Street, checking our watches. His stride had lengthened now, and I didn't have to hold back my own pace as much. He seemed to carry himself more erectly too. I watched out of the corner of my eye as he pulled back his shoulders and hitched up his sweatpants. We'd been following a 1,400-calorie-a-day diet scrupulously, and it was beginning to show. *God*, I prayed silently, *help us keep on with what we're trying to do.*

The longer John and I had neglected our fitness, the more talk I seemed to hear about physical conditioning—on the radio, on television, among people we knew. Every other magazine and newspaper I looked at seemed to have an article about the benefits of exercise for stress and energy and good health. Even at our church I heard discussions. "I'm interested in that physical fitness clinic in Dallas," said our pastor, W. L. Stockton. "There's a doctor there who uses exercise as therapy and preventive medicine."

"Oh, that's Kenneth Cooper," somebody else chimed in. "I've seen his research on what exercise can do for your heart and lungs. It can actually lower your blood pressure."

"Your weight too. It really keeps you looking good."

"All this attention to the body!" said a woman I didn't recognize. "Isn't it a little silly at our age?"

"Are you kidding? Exercise keeps you healthy. How can you claim to glorify God if you don't take good care of the body He gave you?"

The last remark hit home. John and I were strong on God. We believed we were living our lives according to His plan. I taught Sunday school and John had served as a deacon for years. I liked to think we were obedient Christians. But deep down, I knew we were not good stewards of our bodies. I'd often prayed for self-control. Now I began to pray for the courage to make a commitment to a fitness program. I prayed and prayed. And worried. But I still couldn't get into any kind of exercise routine and John was still hopeless.

Then the time for another annual physical checkup rolled around. John and I drove up to San Antonio to the clinic we'd been going to for over ten years. At one point I was alone with the nurse—we'd come to know each other quite well over the years—and all of a sudden she said to me, "You know, Mr. Mogford really should go on a diet. He's much too heavy."

I stared at her. In all the years we'd come here, nobody had ever said anything about losing weight. And now, when it was so much on my mind and in my prayers! After a few seconds, I collected myself. "I know he should," I said. "I'll see what I can do."

On the drive back to Carrizo Springs, John and I talked about our various tests and how the doctor hadn't mentioned any problems. Then we rode along in silence while my mind played and replayed the nurse's comment. Now was the time to bring it up. *God*, I prayed, *I need You in on this.*

I turned to John. "The nurse told me you need to lose weight. Will you go to that fitness clinic in Dallas?"

He gave me a surprised look. I'd often talked to him about dieting, but I'd never suggested doing it on a doctor's program. Then he smiled. "I'll go if you'll go."

I was practically singing. "Juanito, I'd follow you anywhere."

November

Tenth Week: Walk two miles in forty-two minutes

Step. Step. Step. Step. With his longer strides, John was setting the pace for us now. We had marked out a longer route that took us out of town into the country along the old road to Eagle Pass. We could feel weight loss in everything, from the fit of our shoes to our watchbands. I was even beginning to think we looked rather smart in our sweat suits, John in maroon and I in silver blue.

"Well, pardner," John said to me as we swung along, "we've got Thanksgiving, Christmas and New Year's to get through. Think we'll make it?"

"Course we will," I said firmly. By this time, I knew John and I were winning both a physical and a spiritual battle. As soon as we'd begun to try to practice good stewardship of our bodies, the temple of His Holy Spirit, I felt we were back in harmony with the Lord.

I had learned that if you pray long enough and earnestly enough about a besetting problem—of any kind—you are actually exercising your spiritual muscles. This praying strengthens you to ally yourself with His purpose. And eventually you develop the willpower and discipline to carry out what you know is His will in your life.

These days John and I specifically prayed to continue the discipline. Not a morning went by without our asking His help in not cheating or overeating. And at night we thanked Him that we'd stayed on the diet and done the walking that Dr. Cooper had prescribed for us.

John and I had gone to Dallas to Dr. Cooper's diagnostic clinic in preventive medicine in September. After a full day of physical examinations, we were tested by walking on a treadmill while our blood pressure and heart rate were monitored. Then we met for a conference in Dr. Cooper's office. It was not a happy discussion. Compared with the physical fitness of other people in our age group, John and I ranked in the bottom 5 percent—the "very poor" category. The treadmill test showed that the condition of our bodies and our stamina to resist and recover from health problems were abysmally bad.

"I'll have my staff give you a diet and a progressive exercise program based on your age and your current level of fitness," Dr. Cooper told us. "You should lose at the rate of two pounds a week. Five times a week you'll walk a certain distance in a certain time limit. Each week you'll add a little bit to the distance. In four months I want you to come back for a checkup, and we'll see how you're doing."

He paused. "This is serious business. If you don't make significant progress, I won't continue to treat you."

December
Fifteenth Week: Walk three miles in forty-five minutes

Stride. Stride. Stride. Stride. We were really speeding along these days. Our route now took us a mile and a half into the country, past fields with mesquite, prickly pear trees and Retama, to a house with peacocks and guineas in the yard. There, we swung around for the return trip. Gradually, we were working our way from three miles in fifty-seven minutes to the goal of three miles in forty-five.

John's enthusiasm had grown along with our physical capacity. "This fitness program is like a three-legged stool," he said to me as we hustled along. "One leg is exercise, another is good nutrition, the third is spiritual—bringing the Lord into it. You need all three legs or the stool won't balance."

"That's a good way to put it," I said, hiding a smile. Hard to believe this same man had avoided exercise like the plague a few short months ago.

"I can't wait to tell Dr. Cooper how great this walking is," he went on.

"John L., you're beginning to act like you invented it."

On January fifth, we presented ourselves at Dr. Cooper's clinic in Dallas to be retested. The results:

John's weight had dropped from 235 to 203, and his blood pressure had gone down from 142/96 to 126/78. He'd lost 9 percent of his body fat, and he spent eight minutes on the treadmill, showing a threefold increase in his fitness.

My weight had dropped from 157 to 135, and I'd lost 5 percent of my body fat. I also walked on the treadmill for eight minutes, which put both John and me in the "good" category of fitness. In only four months, we'd climbed from the bottom level to the top 30 percent!

Even before John and I returned to the Cooper clinic, we were aware of new energy, mental alertness, and well-being. John's suit size had gone down from 44 to 38 and my dress size from 14 to 8. We didn't get our usual winter colds. John told me that since he could now get his arms around his stomach, his golf game had improved—both driving and putting. And on New Year's Eve, we danced till 2:00 AM and were not weary!

As for the future, John has a goal of weighing 190. My target is 125. And I'd like to work my way up to the "superior" fitness category. John and I expect to continue our fitness program for the rest of our lives and also our diet. We find the diet allows us enough latitude to eat what we enjoy in moderation. And when I feel the urge to go on a creative cooking spree, I go right ahead and whip up a flan, an Italian cream cake, a pecan pie or a fresh coconut cake—and give it away!

I'd also like to give something to you if you're interested in improving your physical fitness. And that's the inspiration to ask your doctor to recommend an exercise program for you.

Just look back over the headings in this story, and you'll get an idea of what a long distance some very out-of-shape people came in four short months. You can do it too!

Best of all, our good Lord is willing to help you every step of the way.

MY ADVENTURE IN OLD AGE by Pat Moore

At seven o'clock on a May morning, I opened the door of my New York apartment and stepped nervously into the hall. As an eighty-five-year-old woman, I was apprehensive about the strange trip about to begin. I extended my cane, feeling carefully for the first step of the stairs. My stiffened fingers fumbled at the hand-rail. My legs strained awkwardly. One step . . . two, three . . . breathe hard . . . four. . . . Twelve steps. I reached the first landing and leaned against the wall to catch my breath.

So far, so good, I said to myself.

And then I stopped. Was I overdoing it? Would I get away with this act of mine? For I wasn't really eighty-five at all. Underneath the trappings of this aged body was the real me—a twenty-six-year-old woman.

I was pretending to be an older woman because I wanted to find out for myself what it was like to be elderly. Working in the field of industrial design, developing the products we all use each day, I'd grown interested in the peculiar problems that some of these appliances could present to older people. Refrigerator doors, for instance. Because the human body's center of gravity lowers with age, and we lose strength in our lower arms and legs, it sometimes becomes difficult to open a thoughtlessly designed refrigerator. Or take glass coffeemaker pots. A good design would provide two grips, to make hot, heavy containers more manageable for arthritic hands.

My curiosity whetted, I had enrolled at Columbia University to study the science of aging, gerontology.

Still wanting to know more, I had decided one day that I would become an older person, live as one, discover firsthand the problems of the elderly and their pleasures too.

As a first step, I learned how to "age" myself. It was a complicated procedure requiring four hours of special techniques that TV makeup artist Barbara Kelly designed and taught me. Eventually, with latex foam giving my face its folds and wrinkles, a heavy fabric binding my body, and a gray wig on my head, I became sixty years older and ready to set forth on my grand adventure.

My destination that first day was a conference on aging in Columbus, Ohio, which had long been on my agenda. Would anyone, I wondered, see through my disguise? I was soon to face that test. My landlady came down the steps, glanced at me, and said, "Oh, I'm sorry. I thought you were somebody else."

"Don't you recognize me?" I asked in a voice intentionally strained and cracked from shouting into a pillow.

"No, ma'am, I don't," she said, staring at me.

"I'm Pat Moore." I laughed. Her eyes widened. I had passed.

Out on the Manhattan street where traffic raced by, I set down my little suitcase at the curb and tried to signal a cab. Taxi after taxi flashed past, all empty. Perhaps they didn't notice me. Or did they feel that old ladies don't tip well?

Finally a Yellow Cab swerved to the curb. The young driver leaped out and took my bag. "Where to, ma'am?"

"LaGuardia Airport." I sighed, settling into the seat. On the way, he kept up a friendly conversation. By the time he gently helped me out of the cab, I was feeling good. Being old was not half bad.

But my spirits were dashed at the airline ticket counter where I found myself in a line of businessmen. "Good morning, sir." the agent exclaimed brightly to each man, handing back his ticket with a "Have a pleasant trip." When old-lady-me peered up at him through thick spectacles, however, all I got was a look at my ticket, a mutter of "Columbus" and an abrupt "Next."

I felt a sense of being dismissed, of not being considered worthy of attention. On the plane I puzzled about this. Is there an undue emphasis on youth in our country? Do people lose their worth when they pass a certain age?

At the conference in Columbus, we were studying the housing-for-the-aged and the nursing home markets. Here, I was in company with young professionals dedicated to the problems of the elderly and yet, incredibly, it seemed to me that they were ignoring the "old lady" in their midst. Simple little things like my not being asked to join a group for coffee. If I had been young, would they have included me in their animated conversations? Did they think an old woman would have no new ideas? These were just two of the many questions I wanted to answer.

For three years, I put on my masquerade at least one day a week, visiting fourteen states, meeting hundreds of people. One of the very first matters I settled was my initial feeling that older people are ignored simply because they are old.

Certainly, I found out, old people do get neglected sometimes. And yes, on that first day some taxis had whizzed by me. But they also used to pass me by when I was a twenty-six-year-old (the ways of the New York cab driver are not always easy to comprehend). And sure, I hadn't been included in the coffee klatches at the gerontology conference. But nobody there knew me in my disguise. I went to Columbus as a total stranger, and I—new to my disguise—had been rather reserved. So I had made a common mistake: I fell for the sensitivity trap. I'd become prickly, ready to believe such biases as "The young don't care" and "I'm old and don't amount to much anymore."

Having learned something early about the role that attitudes play in the aging process, I began to experiment.

One day I went into a drugstore as a meek and dowdy old woman and asked the clerk for a stomach remedy. He jerked a thumb over his shoulder and grunted. "Over there."

A week later, I went back to the same drugstore, only this time I walked in with a confident air. When the clerk, head down over an order pad, answered me with a vague "On the bottom shelf," I addressed him directly.

"Would you please show me where," I pressed with authority. He looked up in surprise, left his order, and even helped me read the directions on the box.

It is true: We—at any age—are treated in the way we invite treatment. And this is also true: Age can give people certain prerogatives. How foolish to waste them!

Many of my favorite encounters took place on park benches. As an eighty-five-year-old, I could walk into a strange city, sit down beside another older person, and easily strike up a conversation. We would just be two people enjoying the moment, the sunshine, the fresh air—without an ax to grind or the pressure that I often had felt as a twenty-six-year-old go-getter. Inevitably, it turned out that the older people with the greatest peace of mind were those who had been through life, knew its pleasures and sorrows, and were content to savor the present. It made me just a little envious that I wasn't a true member of their club.

Gradually, I began to see that most of the happy, older people I met on my travels were "doers."

"Now that the kids are on their own," a sparkling-eyed sixty-seven-year-old widow said to me one day in Phoenix, "I'm doing something I've always wanted to do."

"What's that?" I asked, thinking of travel and resorts.

"I'm learning to play the organ," she told me, "and if all goes well, by Christmas, this Christmas, I'll have a piece ready for our church pageant."

This woman had established a goal for herself, and it kept her going. She was a "doer," like the retired carpenter I met in the Midwest who helped youngsters with their woodworking projects at the local school, or the seventy-six-year-old woman in a wheelchair who was part of a neighborhood outreach program in the South. Each day she telephoned fifteen housebound people to check and chat. She was too busy to think about age—or affliction.

I met a lot of fighters too. In St. Louis I visited with an artist, a woman in her late eighties whose whole life had been wrapped up in her painting. When arthritis had so crippled her fingers that doctors told her she would never paint again, she did not give up. She found a way to tie the brush to her hand, and when I saw her, she was standing at her easel, dabbing away.

Then there were the people who had to learn how to fight.

I was sitting on a bench in New York's Central Park, watching some children romping with their dogs, when I looked up to see an elderly, nattily dressed man smiling at me. Tipping his hat, he asked, "May I sit down?"

"Certainly."

He sat on the other end of the bench and we talked for a while about the fine autumn weather. Eventually he introduced himself. His name was George. When I prepared to go home, he asked, "Would it be all right, perhaps, if we met here again, same time, next week?"

"Fine," I said.

"May I bring a little lunch?"

"Why . . . why, that would be lovely."

The following week he brought a wicker hamper with chicken salad sandwiches and a thermos of decaffeinated peppermint tea. As we ate, he told me that after his wife had died, he could do nothing but sit alone in his apartment and cry. He glanced at me in embarrassment. "You know, I never thought she'd be the first to go." He studied the sidewalk. "Every time I saw a couple together, I became more resentful. 'Why didn't God take me too?' I'd cry."

George said it went on like that for a year, until a friend came in and took hold of him. "You're acting like a spiteful child," the friend had said. "The reason God doesn't take you is that you haven't finished living yet. And don't talk to me about God anyway. He's given you the incredible gift of life, and you're doing your best to make a mess of it!"

"Well," George said to me, "after that, I got myself together, dressed up and went down to our senior citizens center. I made good friends there, took trips to local museums I didn't even know existed, and discovered a whole new world. I began to eat again, exercise regularly, and soon I was feeling fine.

"You know," he said, slapping the bench in excitement, "it's just like I'm beginning to live all over again."

George and I met only once more. This lovely man touched me deeply, and I learned a lot from him. I could tell that he had taken a special interest in me, and it made me aware of a fact that I was to see verified again and again: We never grow old emotionally. We all want to be loved, touched, held. Our bodies change, but our emotional needs do not.

Some of the people who seemed to have the secret of a serene old age were—to my great surprise—little children.

One late afternoon, I arrived at a hotel in Clearwater, Florida, hot and tired after a long plane ride. Sweltering underneath my heavy makeup and wrappings, I could hardly wait to get to the beach.

A cool breeze wafted in from the Gulf. As I breathed deeply the fragrant air, a tiny voice piped behind me.

"Would you like a cookie?"

I turned to see a little boy about six looking up at me. Reaching into a sand-encrusted bag, he produced a Fig Newton and held it up to me. "No, thank you," I said, suspecting that the sack it came from also carried frogs and other boy-treasures. His face darkened in disappointment, and I realized that I'd been too abrupt. "On second thought," I told him, "I'd love a cookie."

He gave me the Fig Newton. It was sand-encrusted, too, but I took a bite.

"Do you like shells?" he asked.

"Yes, very much."

"I'll find you some." Then he put his hand in mine and gallantly led me down the golden strand of beach. "There's one," he said, pointing to a speckled trumpet. I started to lean down. "Oh no, let me." Quickly picking it up, he brushed it off and slipped it into his sack. "I'll carry them for you."

So we made our way across the smooth packed sand, the little boy bobbing with *ohs* and *aahs* at the shells he'd find, I musing about the mystic rapport between young and old.

The sun began to go down, and we headed back. Carefully he took out the shells. "No, honey," I said. "Keep mine. When you look at them, think of me."

"Come to my house for dinner?" he asked.

I thanked him, told him I had to get back to the hotel, and as I watched him walk away, I thought of what Jesus told us about not being able to enter the kingdom of heaven unless we become as little children. Wasn't He suggesting that we approach each day with a child's innocence and trust, knowing that our Heavenly Father will take care of us?

Now, five years after beginning my journey into old age, I have put away the gray wig, the makeup, and trappings. I look at them with affection because I have learned so much through them.

I know now that society often treats the aged coldly, even ruthlessly, and I can provide numerous firsthand examples. It's not easy to be old. But who says life is easy at any age? To get something out of life, like everything else, you have to put something in. And from the people I met, I'm certain that happiness can be of one's own making.

Many of the men and women I met had lived through two world wars, the Great Depression, and into the bewildering complications of the computer age. Sometimes they're called survivors.

I call them victors. The truly joyful people were always open to experience—yes, open to all the inevitable heartaches and illnesses and family traumas—yet they were the ones who faced life positively, proud of their longevity and of the experience and wisdom they had accumulated. Their self-esteem came from knowing they were much-loved children of God.

If I should be fortunate to become a real eighty-five-year-old someday, I hope I'll be like my little friend on the beach. I hope I'll have his friendliness and his generosity and his wide-eyed trust. I'll take a tip from my grandmother, who never ever considered that she was old. As she told me once, "I've just lived longer than most people."

6 SERVE . . . AND TAP IN TO GOD'S STRENGTH

Each of you should use whatever gift you have received
to serve others, as faithful stewards of God's grace
in its various forms. If anyone speaks, they should
do so as one who speaks the very words of God.
If anyone serves, they should do so with the strength
God provides, so that in all things God may be praised
through Jesus Christ. To him be the glory and
the power forever and ever. Amen.

—1 PETER 4:10—11

THE BROWN BAG GLEANERS by Waino Okola

The morning, blustery and bitter cold, caused me to comment to my wife that our winters in northern Michigan seemed to be getting worse.

"Did you ever stop to think," she said, smiling, "that we're also getting older?"

Lila was right. I was sixty years old. I had been teaching for thirty years. Our two sons were grown. Our eldest and his family had recently moved to California's Santa Maria Valley. Each time we visited, we seemed to linger, reluctant to leave the year-round warmth and sunshine.

During one such visit, I received an offer to teach at a local Santa Maria high school, and Lila and I decided to move. The next four years passed quickly. But then, quite suddenly, the last bell rang, the last book closed, the last student said good-bye, and I was retired.

Retirement. I had heard so much about these "Golden Years," and now they stretched ahead of me like some yellow brick road— but leading to where? At first there was much to keep me busy. I had always been very active in assorted church and civic organizations; I joined a new group of retired people. We shared common interests and met regularly. I also enjoyed the extra time I had for my hobbies: gardening and music.

But there were recurring moments—unsettling mornings or afternoons, when even Bach or Beethoven couldn't soothe the gnawing anxiety in my heart. Something was wrong.

One day, a magazine article caught my eye. In Salinas, California, a group of retired people had joined forces and were involved in an incredible gleaning project. They went into the harvested fields and packing sheds in the area, collected all the leftover vegetables, and distributed them to the elderly and poor.

I gathered a group of friends and we headed up to Salinas for a firsthand look. A member of the Salinas project met us and gave us a tour of harvested fields that had not yet been gleaned.

From a distance, the first field we approached looked as though it had just been subjected to a severe hailstorm. We were amazed, however, to discover that the hailstones were actually hundreds of tiny white turnips—sweet and tender, but too small for market.

We progressed to a tomato field that had recently been harvested and plowed under. At first glance, the acres and acres of twisted vines seemed to have been picked clean. But closer inspection revealed glimpses of pink and red. When we turned the vines over, their undersides were heavy with fruit.

"What would happen to all these vegetables if it weren't for your gleaning?" I asked my host.

"They'd simply go to waste," he answered. "They'd lie in the sun and rot. You see, they're what officials call 'unmarketable' produce, but they're edible."

I had seen enough. Standing in that field, I knew that we had a project ahead of us. I thought of Ruth, that good woman in the Bible. Respecting God's gift of a bountiful harvest, she had taken it upon herself to "glean and gather after the reapers, among the sheaves" in order that nothing go to waste (Ruth 2:7, KJV).

Could we not do the same? When we suggested a food-gathering program at our next meeting, the response was overwhelmingly favorable.

We call ourselves the Brown Baggers. And, in the past year we've gleaned, bagged (we use low-cost brown shopping bags), and distributed no less than seven tons of vegetables from Santa Maria's fields and packing sheds to more than one hundred needy persons in the community. Most of the recipients are elderly. All are poor.

Twice a month you can find us, in teams of three or four, out in the fields and filling our buckets with everything from potatoes, parsnips, and artichokes, to cabbage, broccoli, and lettuce. We talk and laugh and have a pretty good time. I've made a lot of friends—people from all walks of life.

Lately, news of our Brown Bag operation is really spreading rapidly throughout the community. We continue to receive many outside offers of help. One of our ministers asked me to appear before a meeting of area church leaders, which resulted in a totally unexpected one thousand-dollar donation. Local truckers have volunteered their pickup trucks and driving services for hauling the collected vegetables to our bagging and distribution center.

I'm seventy-four years old now and have never felt better. Those old feelings of retirement anxiety are long gone, replaced by the warmth and security that come from being involved in a project that's both fun and helpful to others. I must admit that I was just a little tuckered out after that first day in the fields. But the fresh air is invigorating, and the work is rewarding. Lila considers it a very special kind of exercise.

"It's good for the heart," she says, smiling, "in more ways than one."

MIGGY TO THE RESCUE by Mildred Krentel

Restlessly bumping against the dock at the Kent Narrows Marina, near the Chesapeake Bay, our forty-two-foot Trojan looked like the *Queen Mary* to us. My husband, Paul, and I had scrubbed the decks all afternoon. We could not have been more prepared for this long-anticipated visit. We grinned at each other.

Two nonboating friends, Martha and Al, had accepted our invitation to celebrate Marty's seventy-fourth birthday on a short cruise to St. Michaels, Maryland. But we worried they might not enjoy it.

"I like your boat," Marty had insisted. "It's the water under it that makes me nervous."

Checking the galley, I popped a melon in the fridge to chill. Marty entertained Martha Stewart style, so I wanted to impress her. *Prosciutto on a melon slice sounds fancy to me,* I thought. At times I was immobilized by fear that I would never measure up to Marty.

Inspecting the captain's quarters, I wiped a smudge off the mirror over our guests's bunks. I frowned at my reflection; wrinkles crisscrossed my tired face. I sighed a long sigh. I had just turned seventy. I hated growing old!

By the time Marty and Al arrived, arms laden with a birthday cake and other goodies, it had begun to rain. We unzipped the storm curtains and gave our guests a hearty welcome. By unanimous decision, we stayed at the dock.

Saturday looked more promising, with low billowy clouds on the horizon and a bright sun overhead. It was going to be a great day!

We untied the lines and headed off merrily. By early afternoon those fluffy white clouds had turned into black bullies promising big trouble. Quickly, we headed for haven in Shaw Bay. All afternoon the rain poured, the thunder roared and the lightning bolted.

At dusk we spotted two men trying to anchor their open boat. We invited them aboard for coffee. They introduced themselves as Harry and Jim. Marty mothered them and tried to persuade them not to leave in this weather. But they insisted they would make it across the bay in their eighteen-foot boat, the *Georgie*.

"Shouldn't take more than an hour. We'll radio you!"

Sunday morning, the waves still slapped angrily against the boat. Mugs of steaming coffee helped raise our spirits somewhat. Tuning in channel sixteen on our ship-to-shore radio, we heard a faint message.

"Mayday! Mayday! This is the *Georgie*—" The voice broke off.

Then another message: "This is the United States Coast Guard reporting an eighteen-foot Whaler, the *Georgie*, without power, taking on water off Bloody Point. All Coast Guard vessels and auxiliary fleet out on rescue missions. Need someone in vicinity to assist. Over."

We all froze. Marty spoke first, "Paul, we've got to help. God meant us to hear their Mayday."

"But there are small craft warnings, Marty," I protested. Marty has no idea how ferocious the Chesapeake can be in bad weather. A person would be a fool to venture out there.

Suddenly Paul was on the radio, his voice steady, "Coast Guard, this is the *Miggy II*. We are able to assist."

"Thank you, Captain. Radio your location every fifteen minutes."

Paul looked at my terror-filled face. "We have no choice, Miggy. If that were us..."

"I know," I mumbled. That's what I loved about Paul: He was always reaching out. And that's what I hated about myself: the fears inhabiting my own little world of what-ifs. *What if Paul has a heart attack? What if I have a stroke? What if we all drown?*

"Miggy, take the wheel while I pull up the anchor," Paul said in a take-charge voice. "Marty, grab some coffee, please. Al, secure the storm curtains and batten down the hatches."

Both engines turned over instantly, belching diesel smoke. Paul struggled with the anchor.

What in the world are we doing? We should never attempt something like this. We are too old.

As our boat threaded its way out of Shaw Bay, Marty and I fastened down everything below deck. I saw her tuck a pill under her tongue.

"Marty, is that for angina?" I asked.

"Well, yes, but it's not me you should be worrying about. What about those men in that open boat?"

I winced. *But what if something happens to Marty? She's like my second skin, the sister I never had.*

Donning our life jackets, we went topside. Marty scanned the horizon. Paul steadied the ship's wheel, quartering the heaving waves. Al gripped the railing with white knuckles. As for me, I hunkered down in a corner, fighting nausea—and fear.

Two hours of sickening, unpredictable motion crawled by. The winds heaved us up one wave and hurled us down the next.

"This is the *Miggy II*, calling the Coast Guard," Paul radioed. "We have the *Georgie* in sight. Over."

My stomach churned in rhythm with the waves; my body ached. Too miserable to be embarrassed, I turned my head away and threw up. Nobody seemed to notice.

Paul began to bark orders, "Al, get some ski ropes and fasten them to the back cleat. Miggy, climb down the swim ladder and throw the towline as we circle."

As Al tied a line around my waist, I thought I would faint right there in front of everybody. I crept backward to the edge of the ladder and inched down to the swim platform, now submerged in water.

"Al—I can't!" The wind tore the words out of my mouth.

"Sure you can, Miggy!" Al shouted encouragingly.

Without warning, the heavens opened and the rain came, making every step slippery.

Oh, God, can't You make this rain stop? I prayed silently. *Can't You calm these waves? I'm so scared!*

Then, exactly at that moment, it was just as if an angel were with me, holding me quietly on that swim platform. Quiet enough to hear God's words, *My child, My grace is sufficient in any storm. I am here with you. Trust me!*

Paul maneuvered as close as he dared, knowing the next wave could crash our boat right on top of the *Georgie.* When he turned to starboard, I flung the line as hard as I could. It fell short, into the angry water.

Heading into the wind, with two lines tied together, I threw again with all my might, hitting the *Georgie*'s bow. I cringed as the men tried to snatch the line, only to see it slither back into the water.

"Al," Paul ordered, "tie a life preserver on. We'll float it by them."

We circled again, with me hanging on for dear life. This time the men grabbed the life preserver and shouted.

I climbed up the ladder and grabbed Al's arm. "We'd better sit down before we fall down," I sputtered.

Hearing clattering below, I looked down the hatch. Furniture was upside down. The refrigerator had spewed its contents all over the galley. Orange juice, milk, ketchup, butter, eggs, and blueberries were smashed together. I burst into tears.

Three hours later, we made our way under the Kent Narrows Bridge into calmer water. At the marina, our boat friends cheered as we docked.

Tied up in our slip, with the electric power on again, Marty and I cleared the galley. We could almost laugh now at the whole thing.

Marty popped another pill. I shivered. I would never have forgiven myself if something had happened to her. "Are you all right, Marty?" I asked.

"I'm fine, Miggy. I can hardly wait to go home to tell everyone. What other seventy-four-year-old can brag about an adventure like this?"

We heard footsteps and went above. Harry and Jim stomped their feet and shook themselves like puppy dogs.

"Last night you called us your friends. You took us in, gave us dry clothes, and food to eat," Harry said. "Today you risked your lives to save us. Why?"

"Harry," I admitted, "I honestly was afraid to help. But God gave me courage I didn't know I had."

Harry gave me a hug.

As I stood there, my fears of getting old, falling sick, drowning... all lost their stranglehold. God had proved He could be trusted in all kinds of weather—and we're never too old to be of use to Him.

THE POT WASHER by Joe Caldwell

I'm the pots-and-pans man. For twenty-five years now, I've spent my Saturdays elbow-deep in two sinks (tubs, really—one for washing, one for rinsing) at the soup kitchen run by the University Parish of St. Joseph in Greenwich Village, New York. During that time, I've managed to come up with a long list of things that raise my hackles: drains stopped up with peelings and cuttings because someone forgot to put in the strainer; someone dipping his dirty hands into the clean rinse water; the coordinator (who is new every week) snapping up all the volunteers so I'm left without someone to dry. Incredibly, despite my prayers for patience, these petty irritations can suppress the joy I once felt at the opportunity to serve.

My most righteous wrath I save for the cooks. There is a substance called Pam that prevents food from baking onto a pan. That is, when a sufficient application is made. If it is used sparingly (or not at all), a long soaking, repeated hacking with a scraper, and an inordinate expenditure of elbow grease come into play. Except to me, it's not play. It's more work than should have been necessary. Much more.

One recent Saturday, I had encrusted pans that completely resisted my efforts. It was as if the tuna casserole had been glued onto the stainless steel—impossible to separate. I headed straight for Miriam Lee, who heads the program. "This," I said, shoving a pan under her nose, "is not acceptable. It's a complete lack of regard. To be able to spray Pam on a pan does not take a PhD. They've been told often enough!"

Miriam pointed out, as she had in the past, that the cooks can be different people each week. Not every volunteer—especially a new one—is aware of the wishes of the pots-and-pans man. They may have other things on their minds. I should take this into account, get back to my tubs and get busy. People needed to be fed.

I got busy. But I'd had it. After today, I resolved, I would quit the soup kitchen. After all, I'd volunteered for a quarter of a century. Time for someone else to take over.

Still seething, I walked through the basement to put some pots into the pantry. Passing by a table, I overheard a woman talking about a clinic appointment she'd gotten for the following week. A man with a ginger-colored beard discoursed on the need for less rain. A young woman said the tuna needed more salt. A young man offered his uneaten bread and butter to the old man sitting next to him.

I stopped. And I looked around. A month-old conversation with my sister came to mind. I had told her I was worried about becoming a curmudgeon in my old age. "What do you mean, becoming?" she'd asked me with a wry laugh.

It was true. I'd become a curmudgeon, a common scold. It's said that as we get older, we become more difficult. Well, I am getting older. Not much I can do about that. And my prayers for patience were possibly too impatient to deserve the hoped-for response.

Now, in that room, amid the murmur of all those needy people sharing a meal, I knew I couldn't quit. How could I have forgotten what an honor it is to serve? To help those who have less than I do?

What I do might be a chore, yes, but it's a chore for which I should give thanks and praise. I'd been given the opportunity to do something—this least little contribution to my community, to my brothers and to my sisters, to Christ. To serve. How wonderful the word! How inviting the act!

I put the pots inside the pantry and then headed back to my tubs. I got busy. And I still am.

Am I a recovering curmudgeon? Not at all. I can be as cranky as ever, with an increase expected as the years go by. But I ask that God, through His love, will translate my mutterings into what they should be: prayers of thanks, prayers of praise for the simple chance to serve.

THE LAST ONE TO LEAVE by Jeanne Hill

Our cozy little ranch house in a pleasant Scottsdale, Arizona, subdivision was now hugely silent. Dixon, our youngest of three, had packed off to college, and my husband, Louis, had just departed for an evening community meeting. I was knee-deep in cast-off teenage paraphernalia in Dixon's closet, trying to clean it out, when Kiff, Dixon's silver tabby, appeared. She meowed forlornly. She was a kind of cast-off too, a gift to Dixon when she was eight weeks old and he a kindergartner.

"Oh, Kiff,"—I sighed—"don't carry on so. I miss him too!" I had never thought this would happen to me. When two of our children—first David and then Dawn—had left, I welcomed my new freedom. And after all, with a vigorous family of five, we really had been shoehorned into our little house. But I hadn't anticipated the silence and, well…the emptiness, in both the house and me, now that all the children were gone.

Louis had a very busy schedule as a professor of engineering at Arizona State, and Kiff was hardly what you'd call company, especially now that she was moping around all day. The two of them—Dixon and Kiff—had been buddies. At night Kiff always slept at the foot of Dixon's bed. During the day, I could always spot Dixon from my kitchen window by Kiff's pluming tail, an elegant furry flag of silver gray.

Now she watched sulkily as I packed away a green papier-mâché remnant of "the grand volcano," Dixon's elaborate seventh-grade science project. He and a friend, Frank, had worked for days on a "spectacular" demonstration of a volcanic eruption. They'd buried red food coloring and Alka-Seltzer tablets in the volcano's pit, which they planned to activate by fluid pumped through plastic tubing hidden in the hall. On the first trial run, I was posted at the volcano table in Dixon's room to observe the fiery eruption. But though the boys pumped mightily from the hall, nothing happened. Dixon thought for sure they'd failed—until Frank spotted Kiff planted firmly on the plastic tubing under the table.

Even in high school Dixon had managed an after-school snack with us and a romp with Kiff before he hurried off to Chess Club, Scouts, or play rehearsals. He often brought home a small pizza then to share with Kiff and me. So I'd bought one yesterday—but it didn't taste the same somehow.

At three thirty every day since Dixon had left, Kiff positioned herself on the windowsill, watching for Dixon's old green Chevy to chug into the driveway. When he didn't show up, after a while a low moaning cry started deep in her throat and turned into a loud, mournful lament. In truth, I felt like moaning myself.

"Face it, Kiff," I said, stroking her back comfortingly. "You're a leftover cat from Dixon's childhood, just as I'm a leftover mom."

When Louis came home and we prepared for bed, he went into Dixon's room and carried Kiff into ours, laying her gently on the fleecy comforter at our feet.

By the next evening I'd finally finished my job of packing Dixon's keepsakes into the storeroom. I was tired; so was Louis. He'd had a busy day. We sat down to dinner and had no sooner touched our first bites when Kiff startled us with her mournful howling from Dixon's room. "You and that cat!" Louis said irritably. "For my sake, I wish you'd both adjust to Dixon's leaving! That cat bawls all night until I can't sleep, and you've even quit cooking. I didn't leave home, you know. Only the kids left."

I flinched. "That's not fair!" I snapped.

"No? Just take a good look at dinner tonight—warmed-up, leftover, dried-out pizza!"

He had a point there; I'd done a lot better at "family" meals than the orangish lump now on my plate.

"And look at yourself!" Louis's voice was quieter now but still irritable. "Do you realize you're wearing Dawn's old slacks, David's discarded shirt, and Dixon's Scout neckerchief knotted around your hair?! I mean...this isn't like you, and it's been going on for three weeks now."

"I didn't realize," I said, looking down at the strange ensemble I'd come across yesterday in the storeroom and absently donned today. Until that moment, I really hadn't realized how lonely I'd been. "Sorry, honey," I said, "I'll try to clean up my act."

But in the morning my loneliness was just as acute when I opened the Bible for our daily breakfast devotional.

How I longed to hear Dixon's strong young voice reading! But this morning mine would have to suffice because
Louis had read yesterday. I turned to our place marked
in 2 Corinthians (5:17, RSV), where we'd left off yesterday...and I couldn't believe the verse! "Therefore, if any one
is in Christ, he is a new creation," I read. "The old has passed
away, behold, the new has come." That last struck a new and
different chord with me, even as I went on reading.

After Louis kissed me and went to work, I reread that verse,
"The old has passed away, behold, the new..." Could He be trying to tell me something? The old was my kids' childhoods, I felt,
but what "new" could there be for an old, leftover mom? With
my storeroom work done now and no excuse to linger in Dixon's
room, I felt the day hanging heavy on my hands.

Kiff wandered aimlessly in and out the door until shortly after
lunch. Then she was gone all afternoon. She didn't even show up
at three thirty—Dixon's old snack time. By four I was concerned.
Might she have left the safety of our side street for the trafficked
one next to us? She would get run over; she was getting older and
less agile. I'd better check.

I put on a jacket and walked halfway down the block before I
saw Kiff's pluming tail in the midst of three little girls from the
neighborhood! While I watched, unnoticed, one of the dark-
haired girls pulled a doll's yellow bonnet around Kiff's head
and tied it under her chin. To my amazement (Kiff never liked
anything over her ears), Dixon's tabby stood perfectly still. *Way
to go, Kiff!* I thought. *You've found your "new." Now, if only I
could.*

I'd no more than turned back toward the house when what that old cat had done hit home with me. I'd never find my "new" unless I went looking for it the way Kiff had!

But where to look? I pondered that, moments later, standing at the kitchen stove. Maybe I'd start my new with a special dinner for Louis. Why not fix something I wouldn't be cooking if Dixon were there? *Hmm* . . . Dixon's least favorite food was steak. So we'd splurge tonight and have steak—by candlelight! (Dixon always complained about candlelight: "I can't see what I'm eating, Mom. How about if I turn on the lights?")

That night no one turned on the lights nor complained about the forties music. We enjoyed a first in many years—a romantic dinner with flickering candles and sweet music.

After dinner, Louis mentioned his friend at work, Dick Raymond. "Dick's mother is in that rest home near us. He says that some of the old people there don't get many visitors. I was thinking that, if you were to stop over,"—Louis closed his hand over mine—"maybe you could cure two cases of loneliness—theirs and yours."

The next day, somewhat hesitantly, I visited with three people in that rest home. The following week my list grew to five. Soon I had a regular group I read to, and I began to look forward to my visits. I began to feel better about myself. Like Kiff, I had found a new circle of friends—and a new sense of purpose and usefulness. The "emptiness" at home suddenly turned into serenity. For the first time in years, I had time for chatty letters to distant friends, long (and uninterrupted!) soaks in the tub, and leisurely suppers with Louis. I even enrolled in an Old Testament course at a nearby community college.

And so it goes. In time, Louis got an exciting new appointment as dean of engineering at the University of Akron, and we picked up and moved with the ease of newlyweds. The passage in Corinthians that I chanced upon is still working. Indeed, I will always try to let go of the old and seek the new. By the way, it's a lesson Kiff hasn't forgotten either. When we left for Akron, our son David moved into our Scottsdale house, and Kiff stayed on with him. Just the other day, he told me that he caught a glimpse of her sidling up to a high school student down the block!

WHY DID GOD CHOOSE ME? by Charles R. Vess

The thing I remember most about that morning when the accident happened was that I was feeling contented for a change. A bunch of us close friends had been on a ten-day camping trip down at Hunting Island on the South Carolina coast, and now we were driving home, caravan style.

Robert and Stella Murph led the procession in their pickup truck, pulling a boat trailer. Then came the Willises—Eulys and his wife, Laura, and her sister, Ethel—pulling their Giles camper with their Chevy sedan. Selma and I brought up the rear in my Ford pickup with camper top, pulling a sixteen-foot Coachman trailer. It was quite a caravan!

"I had a real good time, Selma," I said. "A real good time!" I reached across the seat and patted her hand. Selma smiled, nodding in agreement, and at that moment I had this wonderful feeling of happiness. Which was a lot different from the feeling of boredom that I'd been living with for—how long had it been? I wasn't even sure anymore.

For twenty-six years I'd worked hard as a machinist at the Draper Corporation in Spartanburg, South Carolina. I'd retired at sixty-five, and while my wife, Blanche, was alive, life had been pretty good, but when she died, the years seemed to stretch out as monotonously as mile after mile of Interstate 26 that we were heading home on. I'd tried to be useful—visiting the sick, ushering at Bethel Assembly of God Church on Sunday—but a seventy-three-year-old man can't really do much. When you're old, you're old, and you can't change that.

This camping trip, though, had been a real tonic. The fishing had been first-rate; the cooler in the back of the truck was crammed full of spots and trout. And in my mind's eye, I could still see the sputtering campfires where we'd sat and talked late into the night. Imagine a bunch of senior citizens sitting on damp creek banks and sleeping on hard beds in the cold air! But it had been good for me.

I looked over at Selma. She was dozing, her head snuggled into a soft cushion. I'd known Selma Mathews for forty-three years. She had been married to my cousin, and after his death a few years ago, we'd drawn closer and closer. There were times when I'd think maybe Selma and I should even get married, and then I'd see how foolish that idea was. I was hardly the picture of a typical bridegroom. No, marriage was better left to the young.

Ahead of us, Eulys signaled that he was going to get off at the next exit for gas. "Might as well fill up too," I mumbled to myself and followed him off. Murph meanwhile went on ahead of us.

At the gas station, Selma and I got out, stretched our legs and, after the tanks were full, followed Eulys back onto Interstate 26. I was just beginning to settle down again as we were nearing the Newberry exits when I saw Eulys' car jerk suddenly. My mind snapped to attention. He had hit something. (It turned out to be a large part from a tractor trailer rig.) Instantly I saw a trail of gasoline burst into flames behind his car.

Eulys managed to pull off the road. I swerved around him and stopped. I snatched a fire extinguisher from the glove compartment and leaped out just as Eulys and Ethel got free of the flames now roaring through his car. But where was Laura? Then I heard her.

"Somebody help me! Get me out!" Laura was still inside.

I could see her face distorted through the smoke-blackened windshield. I dropped the fire extinguisher, knowing it would be useless against that swelling fire, and ran over to help Eulys get her out. Laura's ankle was caught in the door. She had tried to jump out before the car stopped, but the door slammed back, trapping her. Eulys was trying desperately to open the door, but the handle was so hot, he couldn't get a hold on it. I looked around frantically. *There has to be another car along soon, someone who can help.* But even as I thought it, I knew there was no time to wait. The flames were coming in waves now, lapping at her leg. Laura's side of the car was completely afire. She would die for sure if somebody didn't do something.

Cars were stopping. People were rushing over and then standing back in shock.

"Oh, God, help me!" I yelled as I ran around to the other side of the car, grabbed the door handle and jerked it open. I jumped in, knowing the blaze would soon follow, and reached across her to try the door. It wouldn't open. I pushed the door as hard as I could. Still it didn't move. I drew back again and braced my body for another push. "God," I pleaded, "please help me. Give me strength." I locked my arms against the door ready to give it my all, but even before I got my full force into the push, the door opened. I reached my hands under Laura's arms and pulled hard and we sprang back through the door, landing on the pavement. Then there were other, younger hands pulling us farther into the clean air, pulling us free of the fire. Soon people were everywhere, policemen, firemen, other motorists.

When we reached a spot far enough away to be safe, I stopped and looked back barely in time to see the muffled explosion that ripped through the interior of the car. Another quickly followed. Then a third. The propane gas tanks used for camping had surrendered to the heat.

While an ambulance driver helped Laura into his vehicle, I lay back, letting the cool grass soothe my shaking limbs. Selma came over and sat down beside me. Neither of us could speak at first. Then her voice trembled as she spoke.

"Thank God you were here, Charles. If we had gone on ahead, imagine what might have happened. There was no one else to help. Even when the others arrived, they didn't seem to know what to do. Why, several younger men just stood by and watched! I think they were too frightened to even try."

"Well, maybe young people have more to lose than an old geezer of seventy-three," I joked. Selma rather hesitantly joined my laughter as we watched the firemen put out the lingering flames. The smoldering car chassis was all that remained. Even the camper had been completely destroyed.

My face and arms were beginning to hurt where the flames had gotten to me, but the pain didn't seem to matter. I felt triumphant. And awed. *Why had no one else been able to climb into that car? Why had I been the only one there who could rescue Laura?*

"Selma," I said, "God used me this morning. I'm sure of it. But why? He could have had His choice of all these younger, more powerful men standing around, but He chose me."

"Maybe He wanted to show you how young a seventy-three-year-old geezer really is," Selma said. "Charles, you have been talking yourself into being old for almost as long as I've known you. Don't you think it's time for you to stop—and start living again?"

Only then did it begin to dawn on me that God hadn't looked at my white hair or wrinkled skin or my rusty hands. He had used me as I was. Only then did I begin to sense the limitless possibilities that God had for me—still had for me. Age mattered only to me, not to God.

More than a year has passed. Tomorrow morning I'm leaving on another camping trip. Or rather, we're leaving tomorrow—my wife, Selma, and I and the Murphs and the Willises. It'll be quite a caravan.

A BUNCH OF OLD GRANDMAS by Floy Jones

People were already filing into the high school gymnasium when I arrived. I seldom missed a home game, and tonight my two granddaughters would be playing in the girls' basketball game. *Even so*, I thought, *the games aren't as much fun as when Ralph was alive.*

Ralph, my husband, had been a real sports fan. He loved every kind of sport, and together we'd cheered on many a team, from our own players here in little Hedrick, Iowa, to the University of Iowa Hawkeyes in Iowa City. Ralph's dream had been to visit every Big Ten campus in the country, and together we had fulfilled that dream. Now, without him, it was hard to rustle up any enthusiasm for going to games alone. Ralph's death had left me feeling as if I'd been tackled in the end zone and had no strength left to get back on my feet. I couldn't help but wonder if God meant for me to live a life so lacking in zest.

The game started. Both sides played well. But something seemed to be missing. And as I stood to yell when the Hedrick girls came down the court and sank the ball into the basket, I knew what it was: no cheerleaders.

Hedrick is a small rural community; that year, only twenty-six girls attended the high school. Most of them went out for basketball or band or other extracurricular activities. There just weren't any left over to be cheerleaders.

"If they can't get some kids out there, we ought to lead some cheers ourselves!" I joked to the superintendent's wife, who was sitting beside me. She laughed. What I didn't know then was that my remark was overheard by someone sitting behind me. The next day Jim Clingman, with my granddaughter, Whitney, in tow, came by to see me.

Jim and I are sort of shirttail related. My son is married to his sister. "I happened to overhear your comment last night," he started. Then, noticing my puzzled expression, he explained. "At the game. About getting out there and leading the cheers yourself."

"Oh, that! I was just joking."

"But it's a great idea, Grandma," Whitney jumped in. "We could get six or so of the older women from around town, and we could start a Granny Cheerleading Squad."

"Ha! You're crazy!"

A bunch of old grandmas jumping around making fools of themselves, acting like teenagers? Ludicrous! "You'd never find people crazy enough to agree to such a thing," I said to Jim, trying to help us both off the hook.

"Suppose I do. Will you join the team?" he persisted.

"Please, Grandma," Whitney chimed in. "You'd be great!"

I looked back and forth at the two of them. They really had flipped their lids. But I had to admit I felt a stirring of excitement, a spark. Maybe...

Somehow Jim found five other women who were as crazy as I was. We set about practicing cheers at my house, and Jim set about finding us some white slacks and red sweatshirts with a big white *H* stitched to the front of them. By our first game, we were the snappiest, classiest gals in town, and when the Granny Squad pranced out onto the floor, the crowd went wild.

"Give me an *H*!" we yelled, shaking our pom-poms. The crowd yelled back, "*H*!"

"Give me an *E*!"..."*E*!"

"Give me a *D*!"..."*D*!"

"Give me an *R*!"..."*R*!"

"Give me an *I*!"..."*I*!"

"Give me a *C!*"..."*C!*"

"Give me a *K!*"..."*K!*"

"What's that spell?"

"Hedrick! Hedrick! Yay, Hedrick!"

The zest had come back into Hedrick High basketball—and though my voice went hoarse and my arms felt as if they'd fall off any minute, the zest came back into this seventy-five-year-old lady's life.

That was the beginning of the Granny Squad, and we're still an active part of the Hedrick community, though we haven't cheered at the school for a couple of years. We do fund-raisers; we've cheered at rest homes, schools for the handicapped, parades, senior citizen centers; we even made a twenty-seven-by-seven-foot cookie for our local Bar-B-Q Days. Nothing keeps us down. For example, when I had to have my hip joint replaced (for the second time), some people thought I wouldn't be back on the squad. But I fooled them!

I am certain God doesn't want even an old widow like me to lack the kind of enthusiasm that makes you want to be a part of each new day. But to have zest like that, you've got to get out and get going a little yourself. That's why we members of the Granny Squad are proud of the four words on the back of our sweatshirts: "We're off our rockers."

PLENTY ON TAP by Marilyn K. Strube

Rat-a-tat-tat, a military drumbeat. Then the music kicks in. The group marches in formation and takes its place at the front of the room. Tap shoes *clickity-click-click* in perfect harmony. Light glints off the red, white, and blue sequined costumes, but that's nothing compared to the sparkle of the dancers themselves. It's the Golden Tap-ettes, kicking up their heels—literally—for the folks in a Michigan nursing home.

Their octogenarian leader, Alice Marentette, used to lead a group of kid tap dancers who performed at area nursing homes. Her husband, Herm, emceed. But the group disbanded when the kids grew up and left town for college. Restless, Alice asked Herm what they were going to do. Herm had an idea: Put an ad in the paper offering tap lessons to seniors. Alice thought he was nuts.

"You, of all people, should know it's never too late to learn," Herm told her. "You didn't take up tap till your fifties, and now you're a great dancer. Not to mention in great shape. Why not put your gift to good use?"

Alice took out the ad. Seven women, all in their sixties and seventies, responded. They held their first practice in Alice's basement. Membership grew so quickly that they had to shift rehearsals to a local recreation center.

Alice was a perfectionist. Even "a bit of a control freak," she admits now. She choreographed the show herself and pushed her students hard. Real hard. One day Alice overheard some of them talking.

"She never compliments us," one complained.

"I know one girl who's thinking of quitting. She says Alice scares her," said another.

The comment that hurt most: "She doesn't care about us. Alice only cares about the show."

Alice was devastated. But she knew the girls were right. She had been too focused on her vision of the show. She called a meeting and addressed the troupe. "I'm sorry," she said. "Thing is, I'm not a teacher. I'm doing the best I can. I'd like us to go on, but that's really up to you."

"Count me in," Virginia piped up. "You got me out of my rocker, and I'm not going back to it."

"Me too," said Ruthie. "You are tough, but I know it's because you really believe I can do this."

The show went on.

Marie Spitzer had been looking for something to do after her husband died. She ended up with a new family. "The girls made me feel I belonged," Marie says. "And I don't care what she says— or how she says it sometimes—Alice is a great teacher. Before my very first performance, she stood at my side and told me, 'If you make a mistake, just keep going. Don't stop. And, most important, smile.' I came to learn just how important it was to keep on going."

Three years after that first show, Marie was diagnosed with ovarian cancer. Surgery and chemotherapy followed. So did the Tap-ettes. They called Marie, visited, prayed. Lots and lots of praying. They told Marie they were keeping a place for her in their chorus line, and they expected her back ASAP.

"I had to get better and get back to dancing," says Marie. "The Golden Tap-ettes wouldn't let me give up."

They wouldn't let their leader stop either. Last year, at age eighty-four, Alice found out she had breast cancer. The girls responded in full force, just as they had with Marie. "When I finally finished treatment and returned to the group, I asked where they learned to be so pushy," Alice says. "'From the best,' answered ninety-four-year-old Dorothy."

The Golden Tap-ettes are going strong. But they aren't on a star trip, that's for sure. After each show, they stick around to talk to folks in the audience, swapping memories and trading laughs. "We'll never stop," says Alice. "What good is a gift if you don't put it to good use?"

NEVER TOO OLD by Ruth Bixel Miller

Back in January my stepson Jim and his wife, Doneta, showed up at the door of my one-bedroom retirement home duplex for a visit. In addition to their luggage, they carried in a huge box. "We brought a present from Leland (my other stepson)," Jim announced. "It's an old Macintosh computer."

"A computer?" I said, eyeing the box warily. "I'm eighty-nine. I'm too old to learn how to use one of those things."

Really, though, that was just an excuse. The truth was I didn't want to go to the trouble. Once, when I was a little girl, listening to the whir-thump of Mama's old treadle sewing machine, I got the idea I could make a doll dress out of her leftover material. It was great fun, and I even sewed ten seed pearl buttons on the dress. When I went to show Mama my handiwork she said, "That's beautiful, dear. Now you need to cut buttonholes to match and then hand-stitch around them."

I got a lump in my throat. "I'll never ever in a million years finish doing that."

"Sure you will," Mama told me as she returned to her own sewing. I got a pair of scissors and started to cut buttonholes, but I had sewn the buttons so close together that there was barely any material left between the slits. Finally, I just threw the dress down and stomped out of the room. I never did finish that dress, and I never got over the feeling. Walking away from things that seemed too daunting became my habit.

"Besides," I said to Jim and Doneta, groping for more excuses, "where would I put that thing? I don't have room here."

"How about the bedroom?" Doneta suggested.

"Perfect," Jim said. I followed them into my bedroom, where Jim cleared some knickknacks off a narrow table, hoisted the machine out of its box and started connecting cables. How could Leland, who teaches computer science at a university, think I could ever master this gadget?

Doneta told me, "We'll be here for five days. I'll teach you how to use it."

"What would I use it for?"

"You could write letters on it instead of your typewriter," Doneta said.

"I'm probably the world's worst typist," I pointed out.

"You don't have to be a good typist with a computer," Doneta said. "You can fix your mistakes before printing. It checks your spelling too."

That piqued my interest. I'd suffered for years from a condition called intention tremors. When I try to raise a fork to my mouth, pick up a piece of paper, or hold a pen, my hands shake severely. I'm a former music professor and used to write my own compositions on staff paper. But I'd had to give that up long ago. And the letters I typed sometimes had so many whited-out mistakes that they were practically unreadable. If it could help with that, maybe this computer contraption was worth looking into.

"All set," Jim said, then pushed a button. Suddenly the computer screen lit up and I heard a *ta-doom* that sounded for all the world like the horn of a Model A—the kind that had rolled down Main Street back home in Pandora, Ohio, when I was growing up. Then these little pictures, no bigger than a thumbprint, started appearing all over the screen. "You move the mouse here," Jim said, "and use it to click on the icons."

The only mouse I knew of was a critter with whiskers. And what the dickens was an icon? It had been hard enough getting the hang of an electric typewriter. *How on earth will I ever make sense of this stuff?*

Jim pushed more buttons and all sorts of things appeared and disappeared. Then Doneta sat me down in a chair to show me how to start up the computer myself. When she asked me to try, I pushed the wrong button. No *ta-doom*, no lit-up screen, no nothing. "Patience has never been one of my virtues," I warned. "And you might as well ask me to build an airplane than figure out how to work this thing." Doneta simply pointed to the correct button. I pressed it and—*ta-doom*—the computer turned on!

We were glued to that machine all day while I tried to get the hang of the word-processing program. Fortunately, my hands cooperated. Unfortunately, my mind didn't. Lately I'd been asking God to remind me where I'd put my checkbook or my keys.

How was I supposed to remember all these computer commands? Finally I made Doneta write down every little step on a piece of paper. It took all five days of their visit for me to learn just to be at ease with that machine.

"Just be careful," Doneta warned. "If you fiddle with the wrong buttons, the computer might crash." I shuddered to think what kind of horrible sound that might make.

So after they left, I steered clear of the computer as much as I could. But then something about the black computer screen reminded me of the cast-iron door on the old wood stove in my childhood home. I thought about Mama kneeling on the floor, kneading bread on the open oven door. Back then we didn't waste a thing, not even the leftover warmth of the oven that made the bread rise. *It would be a shame to let something as expensive as that computer go to waste,* I thought. So I worked up the nerve to try to write Leland a thank-you note. It took me two hours to get just a few paragraphs done, but I felt like I'd written an entire novel. Then my mind went blank. *How do I print this?* I wondered. *What if I click the wrong thing and all the words disappear?* My neck tightened and a little voice inside said, *Time to quit, Ruth, before it gets the best of you.* I got up from my chair and walked out of the bedroom, closing the door behind me. I couldn't stop thinking of the thank-you note on the computer screen in the bedroom, waiting for me. I didn't want all my hard work to go to waste, but what could I do? Around three o'clock that afternoon I remembered that one of my neighbors kept her thirteen-year-old granddaughter, Kristi, after school. My neighbor had mentioned that Kristi was teaching her preschool-aged brother how to use a computer. *If she can teach a preschooler how to work one, maybe she can help me,* I thought. So I called and asked, "Could Kristi come over and help me with a computer problem?"

A few minutes later Kristi sat down in front of my computer. "Look up there," she said, pointing the mouse arrow at the top of the screen. "The words there are called the menu. Under each one you can pick things to do. See where it says Print?"

I peered through my glasses. "Yes, it's coming back to me now." And with a click and a buzz the letter to Leland slid out of the printer. I looked at it in wonder. There wasn't a single mistake on it.

After that, I'd call Kristi whenever I was in a jam, and she'd come right over to help me out. Learning about this new technology from such a young person got me thinking about all the changes I'd seen in my lifetime. Then an idea came to me: I'd put together a pamphlet for my stepchildren and their children telling them about what life had been like when I was young. The whole family was coming in from all over the country for my ninetieth birthday that December, and I thought it would be a nice gift from me to them. Although the party was still ten months away, I worried about finishing the project in time. I was far from a speedster on the keyboard, and I lived in fear of doing something wrong and causing the computer to crash.

My lack of patience made the going even slower. Anytime I had to do something I wasn't sure about, I'd turn off the computer and leave the room before I got too disgusted with myself. But finally, with lots of help and encouragement from Doneta and

Kristi, I got my booklet, "Legacy," done in time for the party. It was a huge hit.

Next, Doneta and Jim got me hooked up to the Internet so I could use e-mail. It was great. I could send my family all the letters I wanted, and didn't even need to go buy postage stamps! One day Leland e-mailed me. "One of my students has an old music program I'm going to pass along to you," he wrote. "You can compose music right on the computer and then push a button and it plays the tune back. If you're happy with it, you can print the sheet music."

Write and play music on the computer? What would it be like to print arrangements as clean and mistake-free as my letters now were? "I'll be glad to take the program," I wrote back. I could hardly wait to try it.

Leland sent me the program, but the instruction book was so thick I thought I'd throw out my back just lifting it. And I couldn't make heads or tails of the language in it. I tried figuring the program out on my own, but one day I must've done something wrong—everything froze up. I couldn't move the arrow with the mouse, and nothing I typed appeared on the screen. *Oh no. It's going to crash,* I thought. *I don't need this stress and frustration at my age.* I snapped off the machine and left the room.

But as I headed down the hall, the oddest thing happened. That doll dress from so many years ago came to mind. *Why on earth didn't you just cut off every other button so there would have been room for the buttonholes and only half as many to do?*

The solution was so simple. So why hadn't I thought of it till now? *Probably because you ran away before you had a chance to,* I chided myself. "I'm sorry, God," I prayed. "By this point in my life, I should know that if there's something worth my doing, You'll help me to be able to do it."

I called Kristi, and soon the computer was running properly again. Then I called my church's director of music and explained my problems with the music program. "There are other, simpler programs than that one, you know," he told me. "And a bigger monitor screen would help you see more of the music you're writing."

So, at age ninety-one, I went out to buy a new computer. It had a bigger screen and an easier music program. Sure, there were still plenty of things that didn't go right, and that did ruffle my feathers. But I wouldn't let frustration get the best of me. Little by little I built up a whole file of musical scores I could play on the computer at a click of the mouse. The best part was that when I printed them out, they looked like they'd come fresh from the sheet music store.

Then, in November last year, the music minister and I played a few of my original compositions before one of our church services. When we were through, the congregation broke into applause. I knew then there'd be many more compositions to come. I'd finally figured out I wasn't too old to learn, even if it took something as newfangled as a computer to teach me things as old-fashioned as patience and perseverance.

AFTERWORD

"DOCTOR, YOUR PATIENT IS READY TO BE DELIVERED" by Brenda MacDonald

Doctor, your patient is ready to be delivered." These few words set the stage for a drama so powerful, it is almost overwhelming.

As a registered nurse, I have often witnessed both birth and death. And in essence there is little difference between them.

There is awe and wonder in birth. Its radiance is reflected in the eyes of a doctor as he delivers a healthy baby. Its miracle transforms the tired face of the mother into one of joy and love. Its promise is a hope for others.

When we sit by the bedside of a dying loved one, we watch with thanksgiving as he is relieved from suffering.

And this is the miracle of death—though there is grief, there is also hope. For, in this transfer from one life to another, I like to think that some heavenly messenger is reporting to the Great Physician, "Your patient is ready to be delivered."

A NOTE FROM THE EDITORS

We hope you enjoy *Glorious Hope*, created by the Books and Inspirational Media Division of Guideposts, a nonprofit organization that touches millions of lives every day through products and services that inspire, encourage, help you grow in your faith, and celebrate God's love in every aspect of your daily life.

Thank you for making a difference with your purchase of this book, which helps fund our many outreach programs to military personnel, prisons, hospitals, nursing homes, and educational institutions. To learn more, visit GuidepostsFoundation.org.

We also maintain many useful and uplifting online resources. Visit Guideposts.org to read true stories of hope and inspiration, access OurPrayer network, sign up for free newsletters, download free e-books, join our Facebook community, and follow our stimulating blogs.

To learn about other Guideposts publications, including the best-selling devotional *Daily Guideposts*, go to ShopGuideposts .org, call (800) 932-2145, or write to Guideposts, PO Box 5815, Harlan, Iowa 51593.